THE IMITATION
OF SAINT PAUL

The Imitation of Saint Paul

*Examining Our Lives
in Light of His Example*

JIM REAPSOME

CASCADE *Books* • Eugene, Oregon

THE IMITATION OF SAINT PAUL
Examining Our Lives in Light of His Example

Copyright © 2013 Jim Reapsome. All rights reserved. Except for brief quotations in critical publications or reviews, no part of this book may be reproduced in any manner without prior written permission from the publisher. Write: Permissions, Wipf and Stock Publishers, 199 W. 8th Ave., Suite 3, Eugene, OR 97401.

All scripture quotations, unless otherwise indicated, are taken from the Holy Bible, New International Version®, NIV®. Copyright © 1973, 1978, 1984, 2011 by Biblica, Inc.™ Used by permission of Zondervan. All rights reserved worldwide. www.zondervan.com. The "NIV" and "New International Version" are trademarks registered in the United States Patent and Trademark Office by Biblica, Inc.™

Cascade Books
An Imprint of Wipf and Stock Publishers
199 W. 8th Ave., Suite 3
Eugene, OR 97401

www.wipfandstock.com

ISBN 13: 978-1-62564-055-0

Cataloguing-in-Publication data:

Reapsome, Jim.

    The imitation of Saint Paul : examining our lives in light of his example / Jim Reapsome.

    x + 180 pp. ; 23 cm.

    ISBN 13: 978-1-62564-055-0

    1. Paul, the Apostle, Saint. 2. Bible, Epistles of Paul—Criticism, interpretation, etc. I. Title.

BS2505 R354 2013

Manufactured in the U.S.A.

Contents

Introduction   vii
Abbreviations   ix

1. Bystander to Martyrdom   1
2. Radical Transformation   5
3. Enthusiasm Delayed and Restored   8
4. Spirit-Inspired Mission   13
5. World Changer   18
6. Teacher and Tentmaker   24
7. Farewell to Ephesus   29
8. Unswerving Commitment   33
9. Visions, Faith, and Courage   37
10. Commissioned Servant   42
11. Theological Groundwork   49
12. Path to Victory   53
13. The Summit of His Faith   58
14. Still Marching On   64
15. Preacher, Farmer, and Builder   69
16. Accountable Passion   74
17. In the Trenches   81
18. Grace, Hope, and Love   86

Contents

19	Stewardship of Money	92
20	Integrity as an Ambassador	97
21	Motives, Strength, and Weapons	102
22	Costly Obedience	107
23	Metaphors of Service	112
24	Bragging and Suffering	117
25	Jesus Is Everything	123
26	Living under the Spirit's Control	129
27	The "Worst of Sinners"	134
28	The Supremacy of the Cross	139
29	His Pattern of Life	145
30	Sorrow, Anxiety, and Contentment	152
31	Imprisoned for the Gospel	157
32	Deposit of Faith	163
33	God's Glory: Paul's Ultimate Purpose	169
34	Death and Other Endings	174

Introduction

In unmistakable terms, Jesus called disciples to follow him. Likewise, the apostle Paul urged his converts in the newly established churches to follow him. Of course, Paul does not stand as our commander-in-chief the same way Jesus does, but he does model what it means to be a growing, fulfilled, motivated, and obedient Christian.

Perhaps we have failed to seize the robust life of Paul as our model because we have majored on his theology and minored on his character and life experiences. Paul's doctrines comprise the theological foundations of the Christian faith. He instructed the churches in the impeccable logic of the gospel.

Meanwhile, he reiterated that he himself was the model of their behavior as well as of their beliefs, of their conduct as well as their creed. Audaciously, he called his converts to imitate him, that is, his manner of living. "Follow my example as I follow the example of Christ," he said (1 Cor 11:1). He reiterated this command in four other instances as well (1 Cor 4:16; Phil 3:17; 4:9; 2 Thess 3:7a).

Therefore, by God's grace, we have access to a treasure of events and experiences from which we can learn invaluable lessons of persistent, obedient, fruitful faith. We cannot risk dismissing Paul as our model because he was a divinely appointed apostle, some kind of supercharged Christian far beyond our reach.

Nor can we shortchange ourselves by putting him on a clerical pedestal and thereby fail to grasp that he was one of us, a man of like passions, worries, fears, discouragements, disappointments, and suffering.

In our examination of Paul's life we want to focus on Paul as a Christian warrior who wanted to win, much like ourselves. We will check his theology because Paul's theology shaped his reactions to circumstances. Our study will take us to his heart, his feelings, his self-evaluations, and the amazing variety of experiences by which his faith and theology were tested.

Introduction

As G. C. D. Howley has noted, "Indeed, the reflection of the personality and essential experience of the author (Paul) provided by his letters gives us all that we need of insight into the heart of this great man of God."[1]

"You must come to St. Paul with fresh eyes if you are to feel his magic," wrote Ronald Knox.[2] As we strive to imitate the apostle Paul, we shall learn volumes about Paul the man and what made him tick. We shall also be instructed and motivated to find new resources for our own growing experiences with the one true and living God revealed to us in his Son, our Lord Jesus Christ.

Our approach will be to first follow Paul's life through the pages of the book of Acts. Luke's remarkable account begins with Paul's role in the martyrdom of Stephen and concludes with his passion to keep on evangelizing even while confined in a Roman prison. Some secular historians claim that this man did more than most to change the course of world history.

Paul the itinerant evangelist excelled as a teacher and writer. He gave us the doctrinal foundations of the Christian faith. At the same time, he never hid his feelings from his readers. Paul the theologian comes across as someone who struggled with sin, endured incredible hardships, was treated as the scum of the earth, appealed for relief from chronic illness and was denied. At virtually every point in his life we can find something with which we can identify.

As I studied and wrote about him late in my own life and ministry, I was amazed at how such a fresh look at Paul the man instructed, encouraged, and challenged me. Having studied his theology, and taught it many times, I was embarrassed to say that I had never approached his life as an example and model for myself. Digging into the scripture afresh, I found springs of living water that Jesus had promised to give me. I trust that will be your experience as well as you read, reflect, and meditate on these pages.

I have tried to make Paul come alive by telling many stories from my own life and ministry, as well as from the world at large. Each reader can do the same by recalling incidents that shed light on the pages of Paul's story and letters. May God get all the glory from our thoughtful meditations on Paul's life. May this be part of God's workmanship in conforming us to the image of his Son, our Lord and Savior Jesus Christ. That's what Paul would like us to become.

1. Howley, *The New International Bible Commentary*, ed. F. F. Bruce (Grand Rapids: Zondervan, 1986), 1095.

2. Knox, ibid., 1102.

Abbreviations

KJV	King James Version
NEB	The New English Bible
Lev	Leviticus
Deut	Deuteronomy
Ps	Psalms
Jer	Jeremiah
Isa	Isaiah
Matt	Matthew
Rom	Romans
1 Cor	1 Corinthians
2 Cor	2 Corinthians
Gal	Galatians
Eph	Ephesians
Phil	Philippians
Col	Colossians
1 Thess	1 Thessalonians
2 Thess	2 Thessalonians
1 Tim	1 Timothy
2 Tim	2 Timothy
Heb	Hebrews
Jas	James
1 Pet	1 Peter
2 Pet	2 Peter
Rev	Revelation

CHAPTER 1

Bystander to Martyrdom

Luke begins his story about Saul (renamed Paul) not with accolades but with shameful behavior. When we talk about imitating Paul, this obviously is not the place to begin. But we must begin here, not only for the sake of historical accuracy, but also for the sake of understanding and appreciating all that Paul became in Christ.

The way to follow him is not by doing what he did before he became a Christian, but by imitating him after his conversion. Paul never forgot what he had done, so much so that he regarded himself as the worst of sinners. Therefore, we properly conclude that if God could turn around a person like Saul, then there is hope for us, no matter how dark our pasts. We take up our story where Saul is first mentioned in Acts 7.

Holding Coats

Acts 7:54—8:3

"Another suicide car bombing shattered a Baghdad neighborhood today, killing at least 27 people." That television news headline plays in our minds like a broken record so that we pay it scant attention.

Likewise, in first-century Jerusalem the news commentator might have said, "Another stoning was carried out today by religious zealots, who claimed the victim—known only as Stephen—had blasphemed their God. One of the eyewitnesses, who actually assisted in the execution, was a Roman citizen named Saul, who said he was a patriotic Jew from Tarsus in Cilicia."

The Imitation of Saint Paul

How unlike a modern biographer was Luke the historian, who wrote the Book of Acts. He introduced the star of his book, the apostle Paul, with something like a footnote to the major event, the stoning and martyrdom of Stephen. "By the way, there was this man Saul (later to be called Paul), who held the coats of Stephen's executioners." Doubtless Paul played this seemingly minor role because he relished the demise of one of his most fearless, outspoken enemies. Although he did not actually throw a single stone at Stephen, he might as well have done so.

While Paul's job was to wipe out this new sect that posed a serious threat to the prevailing Jewish religious faith, Stephen had the audacity to accuse its leaders of major crimes against their people. For this he fully deserved to be stoned. At that terrible bloodletting Luke chose to bring on the stage the man who would soon take over the rest of his drama.

Why should we spend time with Paul at this gruesome scene? For a couple of reasons, at least. First, because we must discover what kind of a person Paul had been. Unless we take time to do that, we will miss the full impact of his career later on. When we read what he said and did, we will do so against the backdrop of his participation in this horrible death by stoning.

Paul himself constantly said, in effect, "Look, this is the kind of person I was, but see who I am now in Jesus Christ." Therefore, there is hope for us, too, no matter how checkered our lives have been.

Second, because we need to recall our own records, however inconspicuous they may appear. How often have we, as it were, stood by and held the coats of others engaged in some offense against God? Perhaps not murder, to be sure, but we need not delve far into our pasts to recognize things we have assented to that now embarrass us. Yes, there have been times when we deserve the label, "Guilty by association."

Or, as the ancient confessions expressed it, we have left undone the things we ought to have done. We have not loved God with all of our being. We have not loved our neighbors as ourselves. To be honest, we have fallen miserably short of God's glorious perfection and his holy demands.

Because Luke's ten-second spot of Paul in his Acts video packs therapeutic punch, we place ourselves in front of the camera. We take a good hard look at the results and we confess, "God be merciful to me, sinner that I am."

To get close to Paul, we can pretend that we were a TV cameraman on the scene of Stephen's death. We can film what we saw and catch the prevailing emotions of the key players in this drama. To imitate Paul, we recall our sordid pasts, but like him, we keep our pasts from dragging us down. We confess not only the miserable stuff we have done, but also the incidents when we should have acted righteously, but we retreated like cowards and failed to do so. We confess our need for strength and wisdom to be instruments of peace and righteousness, like Paul was.

Forgiven Persecutor

Acts 7:58–60; 8:1–3; 9:1–2

History's introduction to Paul is not a pretty picture. Rather, it's a picture of brutal, vicious persecution of believers in Christ, beginning with Stephen, the first martyr. The King James Version gives a stark summary of Paul's activities: "he made havoc of the church. . . . breathing out threatenings and slaughter."

These images riveted themselves in Paul's mind like bolts in steel girders. Although totally forgiven by Jesus and commissioned to be his ambassador, Paul frequently cited his past as the supreme example of God's boundless grace. If someone who had committed such horrendous crimes could be accepted by God and given a clean slate and a fresh start, so could anyone.

Paul's theology of salvation by faith through grace exploded from his sordid past. He knew by experience, not by a textbook, that it was by grace he had been saved, by trusting Jesus. It was not of his own doing, not a reward for anything he had done, but a gift of God.

Often, those who come to Christ from wretched pasts are the most sensitive and appreciative of God's amazing grace. Not that Paul wallowed in his crimes. Nor did he attract crowds by sensationalizing his murders. Rather, he sensationalized what Jesus had done for him.

He never hid the fact that he was "the chief of sinners" (1 Tim 1:15). He reminded the Galatians that they knew how he had "wasted" the church (Gal 1:13). When he defended himself against the Jerusalem mob, and before King Agrippa, Paul openly confessed what he had done to wipe out the early Christians (Acts 22:4–5; 26:10–12).

After his life-changing encounter with Jesus on the Damascus Road, Paul seized the same passion and zeal he had applied against the church and turned it to evangelizing Jews and Gentiles wherever he went. The prime persecutor became the prime promoter of the Christian cause.

His story demonstrates most effectively the principle that anyone's past, no matter how stained, can be forgiven. Past sins need not block our way to salvation and eternal life. Beyond what perhaps have been the worst of sins, God offers hope and a fresh start. Zeal for God and his kingdom replaces selfishness, indulgence in moral misbehavior, and guilt. Past failures need not bar anyone from becoming a new person in Christ, with new desires and goals.

Just as it was with Paul, the key to receiving God's forgiveness and a new path in life is honest confession. However grim our pasts may be, whatever mistakes we may have made, all of us can follow Paul's courage and openly acknowledge what we have done. Whether we feel like the chief of sinners, or not, we come to Jesus because he died to cleanse us from our sins so that we can receive God's forgiveness and grace. Life and hope prevail over death and darkness.

Just as Paul told his story of God's grace and forgiveness, we can and must tell our own stories to people oblivious to what the future holds for them in Jesus Christ. What God has done for us speaks forcefully to others who need to confess and trust in Jesus for their salvation.

Paul's conversion was Act One, so to speak, of a most exciting journey that would in the end change the world. His story begins and ends with martyrdom. Our word "witness" comes from the original Greek word for martyr. Next, we look at Paul's early witness, his flight, and his return to ministry.

CHAPTER 2

Radical Transformation

A rash of contemporary television programs center on the theme of radical transformation. In some cases, we delight to see how someone's home was gutted and restored like new. The harried housewife weeps when she opens the door to her sparkling living room and kitchen. In another case, someone's body was made over and we hardly recognize the remade person compared to the old one.

Paul's radical transformation began when he met and fell before Jesus on Damascus Road. It was completed when God gave him a total career makeover. The premier persecutor was called to take the gospel of Jesus throughout the Roman Empire. Actually, Paul would never say his transformation was completed. Rather, he would confess that he was a work in progress under the power of God's grace and mercy.

LIFE-CHANGING VISION

Acts 9:1–9

Paul's Damascus Road experience, recounted three times in the Book of Acts, has inspired volumes of literature and countless masterpieces of art. The story has intrigued historians, biblical scholars, and psychoanalysts. His conversion has captivated Christians and provides a wellspring of hope to despairing and depressed people.

As we stand with Paul on the way we witness his radical transformation. Blinded by the sun, we hear voices. Astoundingly, it seems to us that mighty Paul has more than met his match. He has collapsed in surrender to an invisible voice that claims to be Jesus. To get inside Paul's skin, as it were, we cover our heads and listen.

Jesus confronted Paul with the dreadful fact that by attacking Christ's people he was hurting Christ himself. Perhaps that was what Paul had intended all along. Had he seen and heard Jesus during his tumultuous last days? Did he lead the mob before Pilate, screaming for Christ's crucifixion? With Jesus gone, Paul's only way to execute his hatred of him was to attack his followers.

Suddenly, at the apex of Paul's power, Jesus appeared and drove him to the dust. Paul collapsed before Christ's shattering brightness and compelling command. Instantaneously, without a shred of resistance and debate, he got the message, as we say. Instead of jailing more believers, and inflicting more wounds on Jesus, Paul became his subject.

Paul sealed his conversion by asking Jesus what he was supposed to do (Acts 22:10). That's always a good sign of a spiritual about-face. The erstwhile persecutor of Christ and his church became Christ's staunchest defender and the world's toughest contender for the gospel.

To say his encounter with Jesus was unexpected is quite an understatement. If Acts were a novel, perhaps you would say this turn of events was implausible. It was so shocking that Paul's Christian contemporaries suspected him of faking it so he could haul more of them off to prison. It was so unbelievable that he was isolated from the Christian community for a decade.

Paul's conversion became the prototype of thousands more just like it, not in the details, of course, but in the outcome. Out of a marvelously rich storehouse of similar testimonies God has blessed and inspired the church. As we stand with Paul at the gates of Damascus, we wonder if we have completely committed ourselves to Jesus. Such is life's supreme question. Spending time with Paul also causes us to reflect on how often we ask Jesus, "What do you want me to do, Lord?"

Chosen Instrument

Acts 9:10–18

Blinded and without food and drink for three days, Paul only knew that he had survived a dramatic encounter with the living Christ. He had set out for Damascus intending to arrest anyone who was following Jesus. Now, as it were, he found himself arrested instead. Confusion and fear probably pervaded his mind and heart. His power had evaporated like the morning dew.

Meanwhile, God spoke to his disciple Ananias and sent him on a risky venture to restore Paul's sight. Paul's reputation had preceded him to Damascus and the better part of wisdom demanded that you stay as far away from him as possible. So Ananias understandably told the Lord this was not a smart move.

"You must go," said the Lord, adding the astonishing, hardly believable news that the fearsome persecutor was to become God's instrument of blessing to the nations and to Israel. Ananias obeyed and Paul's life was irrevocably changed when he regained his sight. Much more, the world's history was set on an entirely new course.

"My instrument to bring my name to the world." What a pivotal development! A hard-nosed persecutor, now helplessly blind, would become the fiery, determined announcer of God's saving plan for the nations. The cause he was determined to extinguish would become his chief passion, at the high cost of incredible suffering in the years to come.

It's difficult for us to imagine such a simple game plan for winning the world to a new kingdom. For one person to set out on such a task would be utterly unthinkable. There is only one way to success: the individual must be God's chosen instrument. The assignment would be God's, not Paul's. He could never have imagined such a possibility.

Of course, on the other side of the equation, Paul had to be willing to turn himself over to Jesus, who had told him, "Go into the city and you will be told what to do." Later on, before King Agrippa, Paul enlarged on Christ's commission and simply concluded, "I did not disobey the heavenly vision" (Acts 26:19).

By God's grace, such stunning turnarounds are not demanded of all of his followers, but the main focus of this story rings true in one way or another. Anyone who responds to God's intervention through Jesus Christ becomes, in effect, one of God's chosen instruments for a unique purpose. When we say yes to Jesus, we give him a blank check to our lives. Paul did not know exactly what was coming, and neither do we, but we must set the main course of our lives to finding and fulfilling God's good, perfect, wise, and loving plan. He chooses us and ours is to obey and thus find preeminent fulfillment in doing his will.

We have seen how Paul's radical transformation began with his life-changing vision, followed by marching orders from Jesus, revealed first to panic-stricken Ananias. Next we take up the story of how and why his mission was first delayed and then restored.

CHAPTER 3

Enthusiasm Delayed and Restored

Suddenly, however, Paul hit a major detour on his road to worldwide witness. He had begun like a meteor streaking across the sky. Then God put him on the shelf, so to speak, for important reasons, as we shall see. After years off the main highway, Paul got back on track and began his Spirit-inspired mission.

Fiery Witness

Acts 9:20–29

Few things energize the church like the testimony of a new convert. Sadly, in some churches this is a rare event, while others seem to explode with new believers. Occasionally those who have just fallen in love with Jesus wonder why the older saints appear to be so tepid in their faith. Old-fashioned revivals usually erupted when new converts set the congregation ablaze. That's why they were called revivals, because the saints got revived.

After his conversion to Christ, Paul set fire to the churches in Damascus and Jerusalem, with drastic repercussions. His witness in Damascus was irrefutable and he baffled the Jews with his powerful words about Jesus. They did not take kindly to this firebrand, so they plotted to kill him, but word leaked out and Paul escaped.

At Jerusalem, the fearful church stiff-armed Paul for sufficient reasons. It was beyond the church's power to believe their persecutor had been redeemed and changed by Jesus. "Fraud" or "faker" were probably what they considered him. Logic compelled them to withhold fellowship.

However, Barnabas stepped up to the plate and cleared the bases for Paul. His backing disarmed the Christians and Paul flooded the streets of Jerusalem with powerful declarations about Jesus. He engaged Greek-speaking Jews, who, unlike the Athenians, did not welcome strange doctrines. Instead, they also tried to kill Paul and the Christians shipped him back to his hometown of Tarsus.

If there were any doubts about the genuineness of Paul's conversion, he dispelled them by launching his offensive for Jesus in the heart of opposition territory. Paul sprang into action and packed the gospel into the front lines, "proving that Jesus is the Christ." Despite all the arguments to the contrary, he stood his ground. This new convert did not run and hide and wait for a more compatible audience.

The same thing happened in Jerusalem, but there the Christians did not have the advantage of knowing about Paul's experience in Damascus. They demanded proof of his conversion and Barnabas gave it to them.

We look beyond the man's astonishing courage to his inexplicable knowledge of the gospel. He proved Jesus was the Messiah; he debated the Jews about Jesus. Apparently, because they could not refute his arguments, they decided to take the cowardly way out and kill him.

Paul's audacious courage and wisdom likewise baffles us. He shot out of the starting gate like a Kentucky Derby champion. There was no waiting for a class for new converts. In fact, no training at all. Yet he knew the people who needed Jesus and he went right for their jugulars, regardless of the risks to his life.

When God breaks into our often sterile churches, and allows us to see something like this, we know revival has broken out. Is that what we really want?

On the Shelf

Acts 9:30; 11:25–26; Galatians 1:11–24

"Saul! What a surprise to see you back in Tarsus. What happened?"

Returning home unexpectedly generates tough questions from family and friends. Our record is silent about public reaction to Paul's arrival and his answers to questions. But we can imagine his family and friends were shocked to see him, this brilliant student and protagonist for the faith of Israel who had made such a name for himself in Jerusalem. Probably Paul told his story pretty much like he told it to King Agrippa (Acts 26:1–23).

We have to conjecture about his inner thoughts, because being sidelined on the shelf, so to speak, arouses serious questions about God. That's where the apostle Paul found himself, not for a few days, weeks, or months, but probably for a decade. Bible scholars think ten years elapsed between the time Jerusalem believers sent him back home to Tarsus and his receiving the call from Barnabas to help him teach at Antioch. This is one of those frustrating "silent" periods in Bible history. What do we surmise happened to Paul, and why?

Part of the answer comes from his defense of his authority and the source of his message. He did not consult any man, but retired to Arabia, living alone most of the time, perhaps as long as three years (Gal 1:11–18). While there, he received a "revelation from Jesus Christ."

Paul was born in Tarsus, "no ordinary city" (Acts 21:39), which gave him Roman citizenship. However, apparently at an early age he left Tarsus to study in Jerusalem under Gamaliel (Acts 22:3). On his return, did any family members remember him? Any neighbors or friends? Had stories reached Tarsus about his "stardom" in Jerusalem, his hatred of Christians, and his dramatic conversion?

Did Paul question the wisdom of the Jerusalem believers in sending him back to his home city? Did they expect him to find hospitality and safety there? He had escaped both Damascus and Jerusalem under death threats. Would the same fate await him in Tarsus?

No, but he persisted in God's school of training and development. Patience, endurance and perseverance became keynotes in Paul's letters to his converts (Rom 5:3–4; 15:4–5; 2 Cor 6:4; 12:12; Gal 5:22; 1 Thess 1:3; 2 Thess 1:4; 1 Tim 6:11; 2 Tim 3:10). Waiting often tests our faith and obedience more than other trials do. We demand action and relief right now. Paul matured to the point where he could say, "He who began a good work in you will carry it on to completion until the day of Christ Jesus" (Phil 1:6).

Being immersed in a Gentile culture in Asia Minor, he developed his remarkable passion for introducing Gentiles to Jesus, keeping Christ's vision firmly before him (Acts 26:17–18). He settled into a routine of work as a tentmaker, which later on opened doors for teaching (Acts 18:3–4). He flourished in God's training school and we do not find any complaints in his writings about being on the shelf.

Somehow, in Antioch, Barnabas learned that Paul's education was complete and he summoned him to a fruitful teaching ministry there. God does something like that for us, when we wait patiently in faith for his good and perfect will.

BACK ON TRACK

Acts 9:26–30; 11:25–26

Despite his personal submission to Jesus, Paul faced an incredibly difficult future. Much like a murderer who has served his time in prison trying to make a new life for himself, Paul possessed few options. However, his own accounts of what happened do not reveal any uncertainties or hesitations. "Then the Lord said to me, 'Go . . .'" (Acts 22:21). "I was not disobedient to the vision from heaven" (Acts 26:19).

Sounds pretty straightforward, doesn't it? But serious hazards stood in his way. Enemies aroused by his preaching plotted to kill him in Damascus and Jerusalem. Christians in Jerusalem, painfully aware of the terror and havoc created by Paul, wanted nothing to do with him, despite his testimony. The only people who could speak up for him were in Damascus.

But then the Son of Encouragement (Acts 4:36–37) stepped forward and decided to sponsor Paul. Luke the historian leaves us guessing about how Barnabas had come to such a firm conviction that Paul the persecutor was the genuine article. Paul's Damascus Road experience had swept through the Christian community in Damascus, where Barnabas had some friends. Their story gripped Barnabas, who decided to risk everything for Paul's sake.

One person with courageous faith saved the day for Paul. Barnabas, whose middle name was "Encouragement," decided to back Paul, despite his miserable record. Who needed encouragement more than this recent convert going around preaching fearlessly in the name of Jesus?

God sometimes calls us to take huge risks like Barnabas did. We hear the stories of converts whose past records would tell us to steer clear of them. When we decide to sponsor them, so to speak, we know it's a gamble, but we also know that love and trust are called for. After all, what did Jesus mean when he said, "Whatever you did for one of the least of these brothers of mine, you did for me"? (Matt 25:40).

The Imitation of Saint Paul

After a ten-year hiatus, Barnabas stepped up to the plate one more time for Paul. This time he called the fiery evangelist to be his fellow teacher at Antioch. That was no small feat. Tarsus stood in the mountains 100 miles from Antioch. It was a treacherous journey at best. How would he find Paul when he got there? Somehow he did, and he persuaded him to return with him, again at considerable risk.

Imagine the Christians whispering, "Look who's coming! It's Saul of Tarsus, the former destroyer of the church in Jerusalem! What's he got to say to us?" Once again Barnabas sponsored his protégé. Successfully, Paul and Barnabas taught crowds of new converts, including substantial numbers of Gentiles. What a year that was for the believers at Antioch. They made such a splash in society that they were given a new and perhaps derogatory name, "Christians."

Churches thrive and make an impact when veteran believers decide to sponsor new believers. Sure, baby believers make mistakes, but that's part of growing in faith. Without sponsors like Barnabas, the future Pauls in the church will be left to wither and die.

Jesus did not save Paul from ups and downs. Apart from his revelation of himself to Paul, Jesus carefully guided him from mountain peaks, through valleys, and back to the summit again. He gave him his significant place in the church at Antioch, from where he launched his missionary career, which is our focus in the next chapter.

CHAPTER 4

Spirit-Inspired Mission

The Acts of the Apostles has been aptly retitled, "The Acts of the Holy Spirit." At the outset Luke credited the Holy Spirit with Christ's post-resurrection teaching. Jesus predicted the filling of the Holy Spirit at Pentecost. Peter's first sermon told of the prophecy of the Holy Spirit. Facing fearful threats, the early Christians were empowered by the Holy Spirit to keep on witnessing courageously.

Set apart for God's Work

Acts 13:1–3

Led by the Holy Spirit, Peter took the gospel to Cornelius and the Holy Spirit fell on him and his household. The Spirit's story continues with his call to two teachers at Antioch, Barnabas and Paul. The church was fasting and praying when the Holy Spirit interrupted the status quo.

These brothers had a great thing going at Antioch, comfortably ensconced as they were as teachers in a thriving cosmopolitan community of believers, known first at Antioch as Christians. This well-taught congregation was ripe for bigger things, however, and God did not disappoint them.

Mystery clouds the mechanics of hearing the Holy Spirit, but probably there was a strong consensus that God had spoken. Nevertheless, the voice required verification, and so the leaders prayed and fasted with at least one specific request in mind: "Lord, are you sure we're supposed to send Barnabas and Paul? After all, they are our spiritual fathers and it will be tough without them."

Somehow, the Holy Spirit confirmed his call. Antioch either "sent" Barnabas and Paul, or "let them go" (NEB), to obey God's call to do his work. Thus the initial mission of the church did not originate with the church, but with God. This was his plan and the Antioch church concurred by releasing their teachers. The crucial fact is that these two men sailed away at the instigation of the Holy Spirit. Somehow, they had received his directions and thus knew where to go.

Barnabas and Paul, for their part, prayed and fasted with the team of five prophets and teachers. Probably they raised some questions about God's timing. Could they safely entrust the church to others? Apparently, yes, because they did not see themselves as indispensable to its progress. They sensed it was God's time to move on. Their faith compelled them to obey.

Their story stands as the model of all subsequent Christian missionary enterprise. Mission must be Spirit-induced and church-encouraged and supported. Missionaries sprout in the soil of a church that is already reaching its own community and is well taught in Christian life and doctrine. The obedient congregation will be flexible, as its leaders seek God's voice and the Spirit's direction.

Above all, Paul's future was defined by the Spirit's command: "Set apart for me . . . for the work to which I have called them." Again and again, in years to come, Paul heard the Holy Spirit and obeyed. He knew he was on a divine mission to accomplish God's work.

Evangelistic Ardor

Acts 13–14

Flying into Larnaca, Cyprus, from Athens, Greece, on Cyprus Airlines, I settled back and pulled a brochure from the seat pocket. Words something like this surprised me: "Welcome to Cyprus, the world's first Christian nation." Is that really true? I wondered. Well, yes, if you agree that the first Christian missionaries, Barnabas and Paul, made their first convert on the island of Cyprus.

Two teachers from Antioch, Barnabas and Paul, and John their assistant, set sail to take on the world for Jesus. And their first stop was Cyprus. They blanketed the island with the gospel from one end to the other and attracted not only the governor but also a Jewish sorcerer who posed as a prophet. This man's evil riled up Paul so much that he struck him blind, whereupon the governor became a believer. Thus was the church born on Cyprus, now claimed by the airline as a Christian nation.

Minus John, Paul and Barnabas pushed on into the heart of Asia Minor to Pisidian Antioch. Invited by synagogue officials to speak, Paul preached his first sermon recorded by Luke (Acts 13:16–41), driving home the resurrection of Jesus. Jews and Gentiles alike became believers, so many that the evangelists were kicked out of the city. Such became the pattern as they preached at Iconium, Lystra, and Derbe.

However, at Lystra, after Paul had healed a crippled man, the people declared that their gods had visited them. Barnabas was Jupiter and Paul was Mercury, because he was the spokesman. "We're mere mortals like you," the evangelists explained, rejecting their sacrifices.

A violent swing in public opinion overtook them when Jews from Antioch and Iconium arrived and the crowds stoned Paul to death. (They thought they had killed him. Perhaps so, if this was the experience Paul wrote about in 2 Corinthians 12:1–4.) Nevertheless, surrounded by converts, Paul got to his feet. The next day he left with Barnabas for Derbe.

Amazingly, after gaining many converts there, they returned to the scene of Paul's stoning, Lystra, and then on to Iconium and Antioch. At each stop they encouraged the new believers in their faith, warned of hardships to come, appointed elders, and committed them to the Lord with prayer and fasting. Back home at Antioch, they reported great victories for God, rejoicing that he had opened the gates of the kingdom to the Gentiles.

In this barebones rehearsal of the world's first Christian evangelistic tour, we discover their strategy to go first to the synagogues, then to offer Jesus to the Gentiles. We see both abundant fruit and horrific opposition. We see astounding courage in the face of danger. We see teaching of the converts and their organization as churches. Prayer, faith, endurance and incredible physical commitment (they covered hundreds of miles of mountain roads on foot) kept them going. They rejected public acclaim and held up the resurrected Jesus as the way, the truth, and the life.

Today in many countries Christians enjoy settled church life, but in some parts of the world Acts 13–14 is reenacted as evangelists encounter the fiercest kinds of hatred and persecution.

The Imitation of Saint Paul

Miracle Worker

Acts 14:8–10; 16:16–18; 19:11–12; 28:1–10

As a former newspaper reporter, I would have splashed Paul's miracles across our front pages. Not so with Luke, who appears to mention Paul's miracles somewhat casually. What is more astounding, Paul himself never made miracles the centerpiece of his testimony. "Oh, by the way," seems to have been his attitude.

Undoubtedly, the Holy Spirit gifted Paul to do miracles (1 Cor 12:10), probably because signs and wonders paved the way for people to hear and believe the good news about Jesus (Acts 14:3). Paul and Barnabas pointed to signs and wonders as evidence that God had opened salvation's door to the Gentiles (Acts 15:12).

At Cyprus, Paul blinded the sorcerer; at Iconium, he healed a crippled man; at Philippi, he released a girl of her evil spirit; at Ephesus, he healed the sick and cast out evil spirits; at Troas, he raised Eutychus from the dead; at Malta, he shook off a poisonous viper and healed the father of Publius and others.

With such a record any healer's bragging would have been justified, but Paul somehow forgot his miracles in his testimonies before the Ephesian elders (Acts 20:18–35), the Jerusalem mob seeking his blood, the Roman rulers Felix and Festus, and the Jewish King Agrippa. Actually, to say he forgot them is not totally true. He never forgot them; he just did not make them the centerpiece of his witness and testimony.

That was intentional on his part. If he had started to defend himself on the basis of his miracles, perhaps the authorities would have been lenient with him and the unbelieving Jews would not have hounded him. But to Paul it would have been unseemly to boast, even to save his skin.

When we consider that the citizens of Lystra would have made him one of their gods, we can appreciate the compelling temptation to self-defense and self-exaltation (Acts 14:15–18). Paul would have none of that because his life and ministry were distinguished by humility (Acts 20:19).

Perhaps more importantly, if he had placed his miracles on center stage, he would have upstaged Jesus and his gospel would have received second billing.

Simply put, Paul's job was to preach the gospel, not perform miracles (Acts 20:24). He could have boasted about the miracles we know about—and perhaps many others as well—but that would have seriously detracted from the centrality of Christ. "I resolved to know nothing . . . except Jesus Christ and him crucified," he said (1 Cor 2:2).

Although Paul went to great lengths to defend himself to the Corinthian church, miracles are notably absent from his second letter, in which he is tempted to boast. Instead, he boasted about his suffering. "If I must boast," he wrote, "I will boast of the things that show my weakness" (2 Cor 11:30).

How stunningly different he was! We can't imagine anyone turning down a chance to chirp and burble about miracles—witness segments of the Christian media. Yes, miracles were critical to Paul's mission to gain a hearing for the gospel, but they were never critical to Paul's self-esteem. Thank God he is the God of miracles; thank God for servants like Paul who refused to have their heads turned by miraculous powers.

Paul's tour of duty launched him into some amazing confrontations. We follow him in the next chapter as he became a remarkable world changer.

CHAPTER 5

World Changer

The gospel revolution ignited by Paul spread to the key Roman cities of Philippi, Thessalonica, Berea, and Athens. In Paul's encounters we see how the gospel penetrated various sectors of society and what it cost him in some tough circumstances.

BELIEVE AND BE SAVED

Acts 16:16–40

Apart from John 3:16, arguably no Bible verse has been more often quoted by Christians explaining the gospel than Acts 16:31. Courageously, clearly and simply, Paul and Silas answered the terrified jailer's question: "What must I do to be saved?" by telling him to believe in the Lord Jesus Christ.

Among the many episodes marking Paul's missionary efforts, the Philippian affair ranks near the top because it captures so much about Paul. The story also packs the exciting elements that a television or movie director would love to include in his production: the liberation of the slave girl fortune-teller; the arrest, flogging and imprisonment of Paul and Silas; their prayers and hymns to God; a dramatic midnight earthquake that sprung the prisoners; the jailer's despair unto death and his subsequent conversion; and the release of Paul and Silas.

Looking to Paul as our model, what stands out about him in this story? He had a short fuse when it came to encountering the devil. He knew the reality of Satan's dark spirits and refused to kowtow to their sinister powers. Paul also looked with compassion on Satan's helpless victims, as Jesus did.

When he deemed it necessary, he called on the power Jesus had given him to defeat Satan and release the girl.

Paul's trust in Jesus gave him exceptional courage, because he knew the risks of antagonizing the girl's owners. They were enraged when they saw their income evaporate like the morning mist. Disturbing the devil's empire brought down the fury of these men on Paul and Silas. Without any protection, they were falsely accused of civil disobedience and then flogged and thrown into prison.

Through all of these events God was setting the stage for his intervention that would not only spring Paul and Silas but also bring salvation to the jailer and his household. Imagine, if you can, how you would have felt under such painful, distressing circumstances and then consider what Paul and Silas did: they prayed and sang hymns.

Their faith and hope transformed the dungeon to a place of worship and witness. Other prisoners heard them. God's name was honored and lifted up by the Lord's servants who followed the footsteps of the psalmists who sang songs in the night (Ps 42:8; 77:6).

The violent earthquake not only sprang the prison doors but also the prisoners' chains, drawing the logical response from the jailer: he was dead meat. Paul's heart and soul covered the man before he killed himself. No one had escaped. The jailer knew to whom he owed his life and his career, so he located Paul and Silas in their cell and pleaded with them to help him find salvation.

Prepared with their prompt answer, they did not philosophize about the superiority of their religion or attack Greek and Roman deities. They did not rail against their accusers who had thrown them into prison. They took him directly to Jesus and the jailer and his household found salvation and were baptized. God's power in the gospel was released in them as it had been in the slave girl.

Another side of Paul came to light the following morning. He was a man of justice and righteousness as well as a tender heart and a compelling message. He demanded and received an escort by the very ones who had treated him and Silas so shabbily.

Exquisite faith, love and courage stamped Paul's life in the face of Satan's powers and vicious, uncalled for physical suffering and confinement. Through Paul and Silas Jesus transformed hopeless situations into brilliant examples of his love and grace. "Believe and be saved"—saved from your sins, your fears, and your hopeless circumstances.

Revolution Spreads

Acts 17:1–9

Reputations of trouble-makers spread like prairie fires. We avoid them as we do poison ivy vines. Sometimes, however, that's impossible and we find ourselves embroiled with trouble-makers, like it or not. That's what happened to the citizens of ancient Thessalonica when Paul and Silas arrived and declared Jesus to them.

Their reputation preceded them because they had caused such a stir in other Greek cities. In fact, their accusers charged them with causing trouble "all over the world." You don't escape notice—and jail, or worse—if you go around saying that Jesus is king, not Caesar. Emperors show little patience with that kind of talk.

While there's no evidence to back specific charges of treason against Paul and Silas, mobs are not fussy about details and the rioters believed they had enough to make the charge stick. What was clearly evident was the trouble caused by visitors with a powerfully divisive message.

The King James Version catches the drama of the rioters' outburst, declaring that the trouble-makers had "turned the world upside down" (17:6). Jesus had turned Paul's world upside down and Paul followed suit everywhere he went. Nothing could dampen the explosiveness of Paul's preaching.

Jesus said the good news would burst old wineskins and shred old cloth. The gospel would flip the world on its ear like a tiny mustard seed turns into a tree. The Thessalonians did not hesitate to cut the fuse that was igniting their city. The trouble-makers were rupturing their status quo. The gospel tide threatened to engulf Thessalonica like a tsunami.

But Paul and Silas did not storm the city like political candidates. Instead, they followed normal practice by engaging in religious debate in the Jewish synagogue. The ruckus started over Jesus: some believed and some did not. Jesus is the ultimate world-changer, and he turns people, cities and societies upside down when people like Paul make him a public issue.

The rioters' accusation may have been overblown in the strict sense, but their charge caught the essence of what Paul was about. Ultimately, the Christian message did revolutionize the Roman world. The revolution started when Paul, an itinerant evangelist, courageously and wisely proclaimed the death and resurrection of Jesus of Nazareth.

World Changer

Paul's message targeted individuals, of course, but it spread like a contagious virus around the Mediterranean world. The Holy Spirit unleashed a dynamic in the early church that in the end overcame Caesar. Sometimes the church appears to be fighting a losing battle. When pessimism attacks us, we recall the riot in Thessalonica and ask God to help us turn our worlds upside down for Jesus.

Often we can start where Paul started: with a small Bible study discussion group where we can examine the claims of Christ. Only when he is clearly presented can people make informed choices about him. When someone says Yes to him, their world is changed forever.

Paul's passionate proclamation of Jesus went much further than simply announcing that he had been crucified. He insisted on the necessity of his death and resurrection. That's what got him into trouble.

At the Greek city of Thessalonica he had argued with the Jews in the synagogue for three weeks. Like a skillful case lawyer, he built his compelling case for the necessity of Christ's death and resurrection from the Old Testament scriptures. He convinced some of them, but those who rejected his arguments stirred up the rabble, intending to drag Paul and Silas before the court.

What caused such a sharp division of opinion? Paul's fearless shattering of the Jews' metaphysical icon of their Messiah. This glorious figure of Jewish restoration hopes could not possibly suffer. No sir, he was going to rule. True, many prophets had pointed to Messiah's glorious universal kingdom, but only after he had suffered.

Somehow, this aspect of messianic prophecies had escaped them. Were they ignorant, or blinded by the explosive combination of patriotism and religion? Regardless, to their minds and hearts it was outrageous to insist, as Paul had done, that the prophet Jesus of Nazareth, who had been executed on a Roman cross in Jerusalem, was actually the promised Messiah of ancient Israel.

Paul was not blindsided by their hostile reaction. He knew what was coming, but he never veered from his standard approach: preach the crucified Jesus as the Messiah and argue from the scriptures. Jesus had to suffer because that's what God had revealed would happen. Paradoxically to humanity, the king of kings and the Lord of glory had to be rejected, humiliated, deserted, tried unjustly, scourged, and nailed to a cross. Elsewhere, Paul confessed that this disaster was a "stumbling block to the Jews" (1 Cor 1:23).

Paul's later theology inspires us to contemplate the enormous fact that our sin necessitated Christ's suffering (Rom 3:25; 5:8, 18–19). Here we confront a monumental stumbling block of our own. How could it possibly be true that I am bad enough to bring down the hammer and nails on Jesus, who never did anything bad? But if we want to absorb the full impact of how bad we are, the cross will do precisely that.

Paul sets the pace for us with his unequivocal insistence that Jesus had to suffer and rise from the dead. He never ducked uncomfortable, unpopular truth. He brought Jesus to the arena and started a fight. Potential firefights never deterred him. Such was his inseparable bond between himself, Jesus, and the truth.

How refreshing to observe Paul keeping the main thing the main thing. He had declared his allegiance to the cross, not just as a religious symbol, but as the centerpiece of his preaching. He longed to know Christ and the power of his resurrection. Such power energized him when he entered the doors of the Thessalonian synagogue.

Suffering and resurrection epitomized not only what Christians believe about Jesus the Messiah, but also about themselves. Our salvation rests in Christ's death for our sins. His resurrection guarantees glory to come. In the meantime, we press on through suffering because that is what Jesus did and because such is the only sure path to our ultimate triumph. We also dare not flinch from the gruesome fact that Messiah had to suffer.

Idolatry Challenged

Acts 17:16–34

The salon had just opened and I was the first one in line for a pedicure. The owner busied himself tidying up his shop and then attended to his religious duty. He dusted the small Buddha, ignited two long stems of incense, inserted them in the statue, placed some bits of fruit before the idol and bowed quickly before it. If he said anything, I could not hear it.

I did not have to travel to Japan, China, or India to witness contemporary idolatry. It was right here in my hometown. I was more curious about how this shop owner performed his daily ritual before he started business. I was not "greatly distressed" like Paul was when he was overwhelmed by the multitude of idols in ancient Athens.

Because Paul was committed to one true and living God, and because Jesus had ordered him to take his salvation message to Gentiles as well as Jews, Paul felt compelled to say something to the idolaters of Athens. He was not merely a tourist. He was far more than a curious bystander.

Athenian idolatry ripped into his heart, mind, and soul. He was not content to toss it off in the name of religious tolerance or pluralism. Prevailing idolatry made him mad in a good sense, because these idols took the place of his God, the supreme ruler of the universe and the only God worthy of reverence, praise, worship, love, power, honor, glory, and obedience.

So Paul launched his campaign for God with Jewish and Gentile worshipers and with ordinary passersby in the city square. Soon the battle raged, because Paul in effect downgraded the idols of Athens and instead promoted a foreign deity by preaching about Jesus and his resurrection.

Paul never retreated. In fact, his forthright approach brought him an invitation to speak before the council of the Areopagus, a kind of religious and civic court. Imagine telling men of this high caliber to repent, but that's what he did.

This story reveals the depths of Paul's heart for followers of false religions. He simply could not stomach the pervasive idolatry of the Athenians and in response took Jesus to the highest levels of debate, not trying to win an argument but trying to get them to repent and follow Jesus.

His passion linked his courage and wisdom. At considerable risk he took the good news out of the synagogue into the marketplace. There he accepted the intellectual, moral, and spiritual challenges posed by idolatry and spoke wisely and fearlessly about the truth he had received from God.

Our cities and hometowns may not be saturated with idols the way Athens was, but idolatry makes its insidious attacks in other ways besides physical representations of our gods. When the apostles warned the early Christians against idols (Eph 5:5; 1 John 5:21), they had something more in mind than statues.

Only wholehearted commitment to God and his truth will drive us to great distress about idols and idolatry. I spoke no words to the Asian salon keeper about his idol. It hurt me to think about the futility of his ritual and the darkness of his heart and mind. I failed to take Jesus into the marketplace the way Paul did.

Paul was not only a pioneer evangelist. We see him next in his role as a teacher and how he supported himself as a tentmaker.

CHAPTER 6

Teacher and Tentmaker

Equally important to evangelistic preaching in Paul's life were his responsibilities to teach and make tents. His trade supported him while he taught his new converts. His model has been copied by subsequent generations of missionaries, pastors, and evangelists.

LONG-TERM TEACHING

Acts 11:25–26; 18:1–11; 19:8–10

Paul's evangelistic exploits excite us as we read his story in Acts. His long-term teaching stints in Antioch, Corinth, and Ephesus seem rather dull by comparison. But for those early Christians his teaching provided the vital information for their subsequent growth and survival. His teachings in written form offer the same essential spiritual nourishment for Christians today.

Paul's sponsor Barnabas obviously acted in faith when he invited Paul to join him teaching at Antioch. At the same time, his call rested on Paul's reputation as a first-rate scholar in Jerusalem. As a student of Gamaliel, Paul grappled with basic Jewish theology. This knowledge empowered his subsequent witness to the Jews.

However, far more importantly, the Lord Jesus Christ intervened in this man's education and became Paul's personal teacher (Gal 1:11–12). When Paul turned his life over to Jesus, he became a vessel eager to be filled with everything required of a successful teacher and evangelist. Jesus became Paul's supreme authority, not Gamaliel or any other scholar.

Luke the historian chose to record some of Paul's evangelistic sermons, but he did not bother to give us even Cliff Notes of his teaching sessions at Ephesus and Corinth. At Antioch, Barnabas "encouraged them all to remain true to the Lord with all their hearts" (Acts 11:23). Paul followed this pattern later on as he itinerated among the churches, "strengthening the disciples" (Acts 18:23).

He "encouraged" the new converts at Philippi (Acts 16:40). He "reasoned with them from the Scriptures" at Thessalonica (Acts 17:2–3), "explaining and proving that the Christ had to suffer and rise from the dead." At Ephesus he argued "persuasively about the kingdom of God" (Acts 19:8). There, by his own testimony, he did not hesitate "to preach anything that would be helpful to you . . . publicly and from house to house" (Acts 20:20).

To get a firm grasp on Paul's teaching requires diligent study of his epistles, where he reveals Christian doctrine, the Christian way of life, and his own internal struggles. Essentially, Paul committed himself to evangelism and to building the faith of new converts. If we could select one word to characterize his teaching it would be what the King James Bible translators called "edification," or building up Christians and the church. He told the Corinthians that God had given him the authority to build them up (2 Cor 10:8; 12:19; 13:10). God's servants in the church are to prepare others "so that the body of Christ may be built up" (Eph. 4:12).

Uniquely, Paul combined passion for both bringing people to faith in Christ and instructing them so that the congregations would be spiritually powerful and morally upright in a decadent society. Instead of weak, wind-blown congregations, he longed for strong bodies of believers (Eph 4:15–16). Such growth and strength arise from clear, powerful, wise, and loving teaching. Paul the teacher showed us the way to attain "the whole measure of the fullness of Christ" (Eph 4:13).

STRENGTHENING NEW CONVERTS

Acts 18:20–23; Romans 1:11–12

As a new convert to Christ, just beginning college, I needed spiritual strength, but I didn't realize it. I was pretty cocky, enjoyed a decent part-time job, good health, good grades, good friends, and a contented home life. Spiritually, I was happy to drive through college in neutral, so to speak, neither advancing nor retreating.

The Imitation of Saint Paul

One fall day a senior collared me. He shared Paul's mission: strengthen converts. In a friendly but persuasive manner, he invited me to join a weekly campus Bible study group and a daily prayer meeting. These associations not only strengthened my faith, they revolutionized my life by providing a foundation for future campus ministry and Christian service.

Paul traveled among his recent converts to build Christian foundations that would survive the fires of Roman persecution. Paul was not satisfied to see people make their initial commitments to Christ. He longed to see them growing more and more secure in Christ, filled with the knowledge of God's will and steady under persecution.

To get a clearer picture of what he wanted to see in his converts, we read his prayers for them in texts like Ephesians 1:15–23, Philippians 1:9–11 and Colossians 1:9–14. In a word, he prayed for strong believers. So when the record simply tells us he went about strengthening believers, we know exactly what his goals were when he taught them about Christ and their faith in him.

These early Christians needed reinforcement because "the region of Galatia and Phrygia" (ancient Asia Minor, modern Turkey) seethed with hostility toward Christians. When Paul the evangelist first preached there he encountered everything from arguments and riots to stoning—not exactly a healthy environment for starting a new church.

First-century believers lacked resources we take for granted—Bibles, books, magazines, DVDs, conferences, radio and television teachers, Bible schools, and so on. To grow strong in faith they relied on the Holy Spirit, fellowship and worship, prayer, service and mutual encouragement to each other, and Paul's letters and visits. They faced clear-cut options. For them it was either grow strong or fall by the wayside.

How blessed we are to feast on God's total revelation in scripture in our weekly gatherings and in our private devotions. If Paul were to pay us a visit, he would direct us to stories about Jesus and the power of his resurrection life in us. I don't think he would propose another meeting, but he would chide us for not making full use of the resources we have.

Our culture implores us to build strong bodies with exercise and food supplements. We invest heavily in health clubs and home equipment. Paul told Timothy those things have limited value compared to spiritual strength (1 Tim 4:8).

Paul would implore us, "Be strong in the Lord and in his mighty power" (Eph 6:10). Out of such strength God gives us the priceless privilege of coming alongside others, as my college friend did, and leading them to satisfying, nourishing spiritual food and drink.

Making Tents for a Living

Acts 18:1–6; 20:33–35

In recent world evangelization history "tentmaker" has become a code word for missionaries who need a cover. In hostile environments where open evangelism is not permitted, tentmakers secure positions as teachers, physicians, engineers, and so on. While pursuing these occupations, they seek to introduce friends to Jesus. Paul the tentmaker provides their rationale for this practice.

Such logic is a bit topsy-turvy, because Paul did not set out to make tents and then evangelize after work. He did not need a cover for his true mission. Be that as it may, Paul's example provides helpful insights into the kind of person he was. After all, why should this superb, fearless evangelist waste his time making tents?

Twice Luke the historian details Paul's craft. Later on, Paul himself mentioned it in his letters to the Thessalonians (1 Thess 2:9; 2 Thess 3:8). However, in the full scope of Paul's life and ministry, making tents did not consume significant portions of his time.

At Corinth, Paul somehow fell in with a Jewish refugee couple, Aquila and Priscilla, who were believers as well as tentmakers. Socially and religiously, it was impossible for Jews to belong to the local tentmakers' guild, so they had to struggle to make a living. Although as artisans they ranked higher than peasants in the social pecking order, they were looked down on by the upper classes, who regarded manual labor as demeaning.

Paul needed a base of operations for his plan of attack on the city of Corinth. He had left converts behind after brief visits to Philippi, Thessalonica, Berea, and Athens, but he changed his strategy at Corinth. Making tents gave him a chance to scout the territory, so to speak. He was more or less out of sight in Aquila's shop, but not in the local synagogue, where he debated with Jews and pagans alike.

When he took Jesus to the Jews, they erupted against him. But Paul moved into a house next door to the synagogue and lived and preached from there for a year and a half. Many Corinthians believed, including one of the synagogue chiefs.

Later on, Paul's tentmaking labor at Corinth provided significant leverage for his apostolic ministry: he was not in it for the money. Itinerant teachers frequently sponged off their adherents, but not Paul. In defending what he had done at Corinth, Paul vehemently rejected the charge that he was in it for personal gain (2 Cor 11:7). This was also in his mind when he spoke to the Ephesian elders for the last time (Acts 20:33–35). He worked to meet his own needs and those of his companions, and to help the poor.

Paul developed a second major defense of what he called his toil and drudgery, working night and day: Christians must work for their living and not be a burden to others. In fact, he gave up his right to money for preaching, to set an example for others.

Putting Paul under the microscope, we find powerful incentives for combining fervent Christian witness with hard work. A nine-to-five job is no excuse for not engaging in Christian witness and service; nor is overtime, either. We can do it, if we are compelled by Christ's love as Paul was.

We leap over many of Paul's experiences and in our next chapter we look at his tearful farewell to church leaders at Ephesus.

CHAPTER 7

Farewell to Ephesus

We said farewell to our beloved church members and friends in Pennsylvania. Many times we choked back tears when they honored us with a farewell dinner and many gifts. Looking back, I wished I had had a book telling pastors how to say goodbye.

His Curriculum Vitae

Acts 20:17–38

Paul was not applying for a job at Ephesus when he posted his curriculum vitae (*course of life*) for the elders. Rather, his job was finished and he reminded them how well he had performed. Was he bragging? Not at all. He wanted them to remember what he had accomplished so that they might follow his example.

One summer I served on the staff of a student training camp. After one of my teaching sessions, one of the senior staff called me aside and suggested we go for a walk. As he pointed out how I might approach my subject in a subsequent session, I grasped not only the truth of what he said, but also the fact that he had done student evangelism himself over many years. He did not ask me to do something he had not done himself.

Paul was that kind of counselor and friend. What he told the elders was for their spiritual growth and maturity. Humility and tears characterized his life. In his farewell, Paul seemed to say that his life had been an open book. The story in Acts and his letters show that he did not hide anything from his "students" over a substantial period of time.

The Imitation of Saint Paul

What were the hallmarks he cited and hoped they would follow in their ministries? Like a good hitter in professional baseball, Paul was not streaky but consistent. He did not go through slumps, as it were, in which he underperformed. Despite being severely tested by his enemies, he served with unswerving dedication and humility.

Attacks assailed Paul not only from without but from within his congregations. He fiercely resisted these people by his consistent teaching and warnings. He stood firmly on the foundation of the gospel and what he called "the whole will of God." Nothing could or would deter him from completing his mission, in spite of the Holy Spirit's warnings of what lay ahead. Such consummate abandonment to God's will arose from his belief that his life wasn't worth saving.

The elders knew well Paul's record of hard work. Once again, his deeds matched his words. It wasn't enough to teach Christian stewardship. He worked to provide for people in need.

Curriculum vitae read like a list of cold facts. We hope the facts will so impress prospective employers that they will want to hire us. However, when we read Paul's farewell, we sense warmth, compassion, love, and concern. His dedication to the gospel and to the church's welfare shines through the details. With prayer, he sought not only to guide and protect the elders, but also to inspire them to follow his example. What they had seen in him would serve as their model in the future.

When I sought counsel about where to pursue my seminary education, I looked beyond the seminary's courses and requirements to some of its graduates whom I knew well. I had observed their manner of life. I had benefited from what they had invested in me. I decided I wanted to be like them, so I went on to study where they had studied.

Scholars call Paul's speech his "charge" to the Ephesian elders. Technically, I suppose they are right. But it is much more than that. I've given "charges" to new pastors on several occasions. Never have I said to them, "Look at my life. Reflect on my accomplishments. Follow my example."

Paul exemplified spiritual leaders who instruct and motivate other leaders by the quality of their faith and works. His pattern is ours to follow, whatever our sphere of leadership, in our churches, homes, communities, and places of employment.

Farewell to Ephesus

His Humble Good-bye

Acts 20:17–38

Our emotions take over when we say our goodbyes. When I was fresh out of college, headed for an exciting campus ministry far from home, I could hardly wait to leave and get started. "Let's get these goodbyes over with and get out of here," I thought to myself. My parents' anguish at the departure of their only child and son never hit me until many years later when I said goodbye to my own daughter as she left for a missionary assignment overseas.

Paul pulled into Ephesus, knowing this would be the last time he would see his beloved friends. From this highly charged farewell scene we see deeply into his heart and mind and into the exquisite relationship he enjoyed with his fellow Christians. Our goodbyes have a way of unfolding what lies deepest in our hearts.

Preachers have mined many fruitful sermons from the fertile soil of Paul's Ephesian goodbye. Our brief look focuses first on Paul and then on the elders. He was totally vulnerable as he reviewed his ministry. One word says it all: humility. He suffered sorrows and trials while he taught them everything they needed to know about Christian life and doctrine. He kept nothing back from them for the sake of his own reputation, or for good standing in the community.

He exposed himself to scorn, beatings, and jail as he taught the truth in public and private to Jews and pagans, always emphasizing personal repentance and faith. Taking a huge risk, he told them that more of the same was coming. Nothing would stop him from reaching his goal: the work Jesus had given him to do.

Most painful of all, he dared to promise they would never see him again. He also promised hard times ahead for them. Wolves would savage the flock. Therefore, "Guard your flock," he urged, telling them to do what he had done for three years, teaching them with tears day and night.

Switching to the mundane, he said no personal bills remained due. That led him to state a universal Christian principle: work hard and take care of the poor. After all, Jesus had said giving was the way to happiness. What a piercing way to close a farewell.

Everyone prayed, which is always an excellent way to say goodbye. God's Spirit releases our fears when we pray. Abundant tears drenched them all as they hugged and kissed, which, along with prayer, is an acceptable Christian way to say goodbye. Pretending we don't hurt never helps anybody.

The Ephesians depicted the sweet beauty of Christian love. Just as Paul their servant had held nothing back, neither did they. Both parties put their lives on the line for the one incomparable cause in their lives: the advancement of the gospel and the growth of the church.

Loud cries of sorrow accompany us when we say goodbye to loved ones for the sake of Jesus. I have seen grandmas weeping as they cradled babies about to depart for Africa with their parents. Pain? Bushels of it. From somewhere outside of them, however, came overwhelming peace and wholeness.

Paul's experience here has been replicated many times. Often we are called to imitate him for reasons not of our own choosing. Next we consider how to imitate his unswerving commitment to Christ and the gospel.

CHAPTER 8

Unswerving Commitment

Luke never embellished his story about Paul. He chose to show not only Paul's achievements, but also the spirit with which he carried out his mission. Paul never flinched in the face of threats, even though he well knew that the consequences likely would mean his death.

READY TO DIE FOR JESUS

Acts 21:1–14

Christian martyrs through the ages have defiantly seized Paul's heroic declaration and hurled it into the faces of their killers. Although Paul did not utter his willingness to die for Jesus at the martyr's stake, his words have energized those who have been killed for their faith in Christ. When given the chance to recant, they have chosen Christ over apostasy.

Paul's circumstances were quite different. His challengers, directed by the Holy Spirit, begged him to forgo Jerusalem for the sake of his freedom. Paul thought otherwise and defied his friends and the prophet Agabus in the face of what he knew would befall him.

Was this strong resolution, or reckless abandon? Paul's determination arose from his own sense of obedience to what he was convinced was God's will. This was consistent with his passion for Jesus and the gospel. Likewise, he never dodged danger and willingly put his life on the line to bring people to faith in Christ. His catalogue of suffering shames us.

Therefore, he does not surprise us when he professes his readiness to be imprisoned and die for Jesus. What does surprise us is his steely resolve not to be deterred from his mission. Persistent urging at Tyre and dramatic prophesy at Caesarea together formed a powerful red light. "Stop, stop, stop!" it seemed to warn.

Such emotional begging and imploring racked Paul's heart and soul. But he remained steadfast because Jerusalem had captured him. There was no changing course now.

I once heard a series of sermons on Paul's mistakes and this, according to the preacher, was a big one. We cannot claim Paul was infallible; only Jesus was perfect. Looking at the circumstances, we can make a case for unwise stubbornness. What we can't do is look into Paul's heart. Previously, he had listened closely to the Holy Spirit. It appears now that the Spirit told him one thing and his friends another. Was this a test of Paul's obedience to Christ?

However we take it, we can only say that Paul's resolve tells us unmistakably what kind of person he was. When he told the Galatians that he had been crucified with Christ, he was not blowing smoke. When he met Jesus, Paul surrendered his life to him. Therefore, severe warnings about terrible things to come meant nothing when it came to following Jesus. To be sure, Paul was bound in Jerusalem but his lips were not bound. He bravely spoke his witness to the highest authorities.

It is useless to speculate what might have happened if Paul had not gone to Jerusalem. Pragmatically, we could say he would have had a longer, wider work of evangelism. But obedience to Christ cannot be measured simply in terms of work accomplished. Paul's own peace prevailed as he packed his bags and took the road to Jerusalem.

Rather than debate whether or not Paul made a mistake, we can more profitably focus on what it means to be ready to die for Jesus. Perhaps most of us will never have to choose between staying alive and affirming our allegiance to Jesus, but every day we make similar choices. Shall it be what I want, or what Jesus wants? Is there anything I can give up for him?

Testimony under Fire

Acts 22–26

Paul's appearance in Jerusalem after some twelve years of itinerant preaching and teaching throughout what is now Greece and Turkey ignited a firestorm of protest, anger, and hatred. In the cause of religious preservation, certain elements of Judaism determined to destroy him. They saw Paul as their archenemy because he had apparently undercut the foundation of their faith.

Thwarted in their attempts to kill him, Paul's enemies were forced by their Roman overlords to listen to his testimony. Paul gave a remarkably detailed report of his conversion, including how devoted he had been to the destruction of the early Christians. His miserable confession ought to have scored a few points.

Regardless of how dedicated he was to the cause of ultra-conservative Judaism, Paul had to admit that he had been accosted by Jesus of Nazareth. He fell under the spell of this man, whom he called "Lord." In his vision of Jesus, Paul had received new marching orders, sending him to the Gentiles.

"Gentiles" lit the fuse of a furious explosion as foes in the audience screamed for Paul's death. The Roman centurion saved his life and later gave Paul the chance to testify before the top Jews. This time Paul did not tell his conversion story. Instead, he focused on one issue: the hope of the resurrection. That set off a fierce debate among the two leading parties in Judaism, the Pharisees and the Sadducees. Their argument grew so violent that once again the centurion intervened and ordered his troops to pull Paul to safety.

Apparently Paul had decided it was pointless to tell his conversion story again. He knew the Jews lacked credible evidence against him and that there was no legal justification for his arrest. However, the Romans were in charge—not the Jews—and this fact dictated Paul's strategies.

Paul did not try to whitewash his conspicuous behavior towards Christians, even confessing his hand in the killing of Stephen. But ultimately Jesus prevailed. How could he possibly explain such a revolution in his life? The Pharisees speculated that he had seen an angel or a ghost. Certainly not Jesus of Nazareth.

As many others on trial for their lives have discovered, logic and truth do not prevail in the face of enraged mobs. Paul stood firmly for truth in the face of blind savagery. He used his Roman citizenship to gain a hearing for the gospel. He played to the open sore between the Pharisees and Sadducees.

Paul demonstrated remarkable faith, courage and wisdom in giving his testimony under fire. He gained valuable time and was given a chance to witness before Governor Felix, who was well informed about the Christian movement. Interestingly, Paul returned to the hope of the resurrection and said this was the issue in his trial.

The Imitation of Saint Paul

Paul might have picked on many other debatable issues between Jews and Christians, but apparently he saw value in pressing this crucial doctrine. Perhaps in the modern context of religious debate Christians have not given sufficient attention to Christ's resurrection as a unique Christian article of their faith.

Unflinching courage, unshakable dedication to the truth, and confident hope in the resurrection stand out in Paul's testimonies under fire. He set a high standard for Christians to follow. Next, we will observe how God spoke directly to Paul and how he responded with faith and courage.

CHAPTER 9

Visions, Faith, and Courage

Since the days of Paul, church history has been filled with stories about God's revealing himself in visions. Some have proved bogus, others real. But there's no debate about the validity of faith and courage at all times and in all circumstances.

God Spoke Directly

Acts 9:1–6; 16:9–10; 18:9; 23:11; 27:23–24

Visions crop up throughout the Old Testament as God's customary way of getting through to people. Not so in the New Testament, except for the birth accounts of Jesus, the expansion of the early church, and Revelation. Paul seemed reluctant to talk about his own, saying they were nothing to brag about (2 Cor 12:1). We might feel the opposite way.

Visions have the distinct advantage of direct communication from God. You cannot miss the point of what you are supposed to do. Often Old Testament worthies were scared to death by a vision of the Lord, which is quite understandable. However, in Paul's case he seems not to have been surprised that God spoke to him directly.

That's probably because after Jesus had stopped him in his tracks, nothing would shock him. However, after his initial vision of Jesus, Paul's visions gave him comfort, courage, and new directions. He took the gospel into Western Europe because of a vision. In the midst of threats to his life at Corinth, God told him not to be afraid. Saved from violent attackers in Jerusalem, he was told to be courageous because he was going to testify to

Jesus in Rome. Faced with shipwreck and death, Paul was assured he would live to see Rome.

In what may have been a vision, or reality, Paul glimpsed the third heaven and heard "inexpressible things" that he could not repeat (2 Cor 12:4). On the other hand, Jesus told John to write down what he saw (Rev 1:11). Our curiosity about heaven longs to be satisfied. If only Paul had revealed what he saw.

Obviously, Paul and John were special cases and we tread on thin ice if we try to use their visions as something we should seek. Dreams and visions can be notoriously unreliable, even dangerous. Spurious cults have arisen from supposed visions from God.

Paul was God's special servant sent on a unique mission by Jesus. In effect, he and his fellow evangelists opened the Western world to the gospel. God's special emissary needed to hear from him because he could not see clearly the way ahead and because his way was mined by fierce opponents who sought his life.

Paul's visions stand out like brilliant beams piercing the darkness of his soul. Fear could easily have paralyzed his mission. Discouragement could have throttled his forthright—and subversive—preaching. So we praise God for every intervention in his life by a vision.

Where do we go for hope, courage, and direction? To the Holy Spirit who guides us in prayer and in scripture. We cannot audibly hear God speak, but he speaks just as powerfully and clearly to our hearts and minds by his Spirit. Jesus promised such guidance, hope, and peace.

Paul said we walk by faith, not by sight (2 Cor 5:7), which includes visions. This is not to say that God cannot speak that way if it pleases him to do so. But spending more time in unhurried prayer and meditation in the Bible provides us more than sufficient guidance and courage.

Indomitable Faith

Acts 27:13–44, 2 Corinthians 11:25

Paul's eagerness to preach the gospel in Rome found its fulfillment after two years' imprisonment in Caesarea and a horrendous voyage across the storm-thrashed Mediterranean Sea. The spellbinding details were crafted by Luke, Paul's traveling companion.

Visions, Faith, and Courage

A very instructive picture of Paul emerges from the crisis at sea while headed for Rome. In simple terms, he displayed an amazing combination of spiritual and practical skills. Because of his experience at sea, he warned the crew not to sail on from Crete in the face of strong winds. They disregarded his counsel and ran into a hurricane.

Having had his advice disregarded by the ship's captain, Paul stood his ground when it appeared that disaster was imminent. After two weeks of useless effort in the face of the gale, everyone's hopes began to fade, including Paul's. But then God told him to control himself, show some courage, and get over his fear. They would make it alive, even after a shipwreck, and Paul would appear before the emperor.

Paul assumed authority over the crew and passengers, 276 in all, including prisoners. He thwarted the attempt of the sailors to abandon ship. He directed everyone to eat and gave thanks for his meal in front of them. After the ship ran aground, the soldiers wanted to kill their prisoners, but Paul's presence on board saved them, thanks to a friendly centurion.

God demonstrated his hand of mercy and power on his ambassador to Rome. First, on Malta, he saved Paul from a viper's bite and then he empowered Paul to heal the sick. The man headed for a certain watery grave thus became the savior of many people. No wonder when Paul finally landed in Italy he gave thanks to God and took courage.

God did not exempt the apostle from harrowing experiences. Paul did more than hang on for dear life. He exhibited great poise and confidence, which grew out of his conviction that nothing could separate him from God's love. Obviously, he kept speaking to God and listening for his answer while the ship foundered. Even if he went down with the ship, he knew he would enter Christ's presence.

Ten minutes with Paul in the midst of this trauma would have convinced us that he was an unusually strong person. Not in the physical sense, but in the realm of the spirit, showing remarkable morality, tenacity, courage, bold leadership, and love for the captain, crew, centurion, and the governor of Malta.

Of course, fear gripped him, too, but somehow he kept in touch with Jesus in the midst of terrible darkness, howling wind, and crashing waves. He controlled his anger when his advice was flouted and he did not pout with an "I told you so" attitude. Everything that could have possibly gone wrong, did go wrong, and his ship crashed and was pounded to pieces. Somehow Paul made it ashore and his prophecy was fulfilled.

We take away something special about this man. This frightening experience could have been avoided, had he listened to his friends at Ephesus and to Agabus the prophet. Or he could have bribed Felix the governor and been freed.

But Paul faced danger head-on, supremely confident that Jesus would not back away from his promises. His mission, which was Christ's mission, called for him to testify to Rome. How Paul must have agonized at sea when it appeared all was lost. Would God's word come true? Would his life be spared?

When he needed it most, Paul's years of strict obedience and discipline in the face of opposition came to his rescue. Prayer, praise, thanksgiving, and worship stamped his life indelibly. Those habits gave him what he needed in the wild sea.

Spiritual discipline is the best way to prepare for life-threatening engagements. Courage and faith grow so that we draw on what we need in emergencies. God's word touches us exactly when we hit bottom. He rescues us from the pit of fear and plants our feet on solid ground.

Courageous Confronter

Acts 28:16–31

Explaining, imploring and confronting—that's the last we see of Paul as he waited two years in Rome for his trial. Consider his alternatives: sulking, complaining, seeking revenge against the Jews, and second-guessing. "If only I had done so and so, I would not be here."

His circumstances were relatively comfortable. He was under what we might call house arrest and lived with a permanent guard. Ever the evangelist, Paul seized his advantage and invited local Jewish leaders. The power of his commission from Jesus enabled him to risk fresh charges from his accusers in Jerusalem.

He explained that he was in chains for the sake of the hope of Israel, thanks to the fierce opposition of his fellow Jews in Judea. Although no one had had anything good to say about this new Christian sect, as far as the Roman Jews were concerned, they had never heard of Paul's entanglement with the Jews in Jerusalem. They agreed to hear him out.

Paul never failed to stride through an open door for the gospel. He gave his large Roman audience his best shot, but won few converts. He had,

Visions, Faith, and Courage

in effect, invited them to Jesus and his kingdom, but most of the Romans refused to enter.

His parting words must have stung them like a hornet's attack. Paul picked up their own Bible as his weapon and quoted Isaiah's prophecy to the effect that even God's special people would turn their backs on his mercy and grace. Spiritually, their ears were plugged, their eyes blinded, and their hearts overwhelmed with fat. All their avenues to spiritual reception of God's truth were blocked.

What must have jarred the Jews even more was Paul's announcement that the Gentiles would listen to the gospel and be saved. How courageously forthright he was to assault the sensibilities of his own brethren after the flesh.

Luke did not see fit to record the Jews' reaction. Apparently they caused no trouble with the authorities. Two years passed without anyone appearing from Jerusalem to press charges against him. For two years he evangelized Rome without any difficulties.

Thus once again God kept his word to Paul. At least four years earlier, after Paul had barely escaped a Jerusalem lynching, God had told him not to be afraid because one day he would speak the truth in Rome (Acts 23:11). Paul had clung to God's promise like a drowning man hugging a life ring. His faith had sustained him through his fiery trials.

Paul's remarkable ability to speak for Jesus instead of retreating into self-pity shows us how almost any dark situation can be turned to light. He never quit. He did not demand a break. God gave him a degree of physical reprieve, but the pressure of facing the critical, death-demanding Jews never ceased. Any day he might be called before Caesar and sentenced to death.

Perhaps more than anything else, we can appreciate and apply the way he used the Old Testament to diagnose the spiritual condition of unbelievers. Paul was so sharp that he knew exactly what prophecy to use for this unique audience. He risked being set upon for offering God's grace to the Gentiles. But his commitment to God's truth never wavered.

It's almost as though Paul said to himself, "What have I got to lose? Jesus brought me here through shipwreck and I'm going all out for him." His attitude helps us in similar circumstances.

In subsequent chapters we look into Paul's own writings, first looking at Romans. We have the significant advantage of listening to his own words, as it were, as he writes to new Christians not only about their faith, but also his. His letters provide abundant guidance as we seek to imitate him.

CHAPTER 10

Commissioned Servant

Having concluded Paul's life story written by Luke, we move on to his own words and testimony about his calling and his message, beginning with his letter to the church at Rome. Romans is one of his earlier letters and although it is packed with heavy duty theology, Paul in chapter 1 tells us clearly how he regarded himself. As Christ's servant he was determined to be faithful to Christ's commission and to the gospel, of which he said he was not ashamed but rather eager to spread in Rome.

CHRIST'S SERVANT

Romans 1:1

Titles carry clout with us. For example, we esteem more highly the one who says, "I am the president of Harvard University" than we do the one who says, "I'm a janitor at Harvard."

In this light, how do we regard "servant"? Paul's distinguished pedigree could easily have merited honors and a title (Phil 3:4–6). His remarkable achievements and his incredible hardships as the inveterate apostle to the Gentiles certainly warranted some honorific address. However, when he took up pen and ink he chose to call himself a servant—not a flattering appellation to say the least. Never was he "Dr. Paul" to his audiences.

But much more than humility lies behind Paul's description of himself. Letter writers normally used titles to convey authority so their words would be heeded by their readers. In those days, such designations came as part of their greetings. Authorities normally did not wait until the end of their letters to affix their titles.

Commissioned Servant

Jesus claimed all rights to Paul. He was Paul's master and Paul was his servant. In this case, however, Paul served the Lord of the universe. He was not just another public figure. Therefore, Paul declared that he stood in for Jesus as his representative, as his sent one, his messenger, his mouthpiece, his apostle. Paul served to do the bidding of Jesus. He was not his own person. Whatever Paul did, he was at the beck and call of Jesus. Such devotion became the heartbeat of his life.

Paul's obedience to Jesus centered on his telling the good news about him wherever he went in both pagan and Jewish environments. Regardless of the setting and the risks, Paul conscientiously urged people to repent and turn to Christ. As Christ's servant, he saw himself earning Christ's suffering (Phil 3:10).

Serving Jesus was Paul's calling because Jesus himself had told him what his mission in life was supposed to be (Acts 26:15–18). Paul never flagged in his enthusiastic response. Jesus had commanded him and that was enough.

For Paul, being Christ's servant meant doing all he could to flesh out Christ's fundamental role of servanthood. Because Jesus lived in him, the old pugnacious Paul had to go, replaced by Christ's love and compassion.

At the same time, Paul as a servant did not back off from confrontation when it was needed, just as Jesus had not. Although Paul was treated shamelessly on some occasions, he never appeared to be a doormat. His personality was much too robust for that. As he said, he was willing to become all things to all people so that he might save some. That statement, and not weakness, pictures the strength of his role as a servant.

Christianity is so radical that its great leaders have always been servants, not tyrants. Jesus said he did not come to be served, but to serve, even to the giving of his life. Paul followed his master in this regard.

Our encounters with Jesus may not be as dramatic and specific as Paul's was, but we can be just as sure as he was about how we are supposed to obey Jesus. Serving Jesus takes as many forms as there are vocations. Every vocation, every task carries significance when performed as service to Jesus. How crucial it is, then, to take time to listen to what Jesus has to say to us.

Privileged Commission

Romans 1:1–6

After banging around several jobs following college, and finding nothing that seemed to fit, a friend of mine decided to become a Marine Corps pilot. His road to that commission took him through the most grueling physical and mental tests of his life. After completing his excruciating officers' training course, he returned home and we partied with his friends and family who had prayed him through his ordeal.

Paul never partied after he was commissioned by Jesus, but something akin to a party took place when Ananias rescued him from blindness after his encounter with Jesus on Damascus Road. Paul became the apostle of joy, faith, and courage without parties, but with strong prayer support and fellowship.

If Jesus had given Paul officer's bars to wear after his commissioning, he would have gladly pinned them to his tunic. However, without anything resembling military insignia, or even a tiny cross around his neck, Paul proudly bore the most glorious insignia of all: the suffering of Jesus. His privileged commission came from the one whose death he daily bore in his own body. He claimed no higher privilege than suffering for Jesus.

Paul's inestimable privilege issued not from rank but from heaven itself. He had heard from God himself, incarnate in the person of Jesus of Nazareth. Jesus uttered his name. Paul stopped in his tracks and submitted to Christ's commission, not fully understanding all this would mean.

That prodigious step of faith dominated his life from there on. For him, faith was not dewy-eyed optimism, but rock solid confidence in the one who had commissioned him. He proudly enlisted, as it were, in the name of Jesus. No other name under heaven could claim such joyful obedience. He marched into battle carrying the flag of "Jesus! The name high over all, In hell or earth, or sky; Angels and men before it fall, And devils fear and fly, And devils fear and fly" (Charles Wesley).

Newly commissioned officers know they risk warfare and possible death. Paul sensed the same thing. He fought to bring people to faith and obedience under the lordship of Christ. He waged war in the most monumental battle of all, the cosmic contest with Satan for the souls of humans everywhere. Paul's engagement encompassed the whole world, all nations.

Paul's commissioning by Jesus drove him through the same kinds of tests endured by my Marine friend. Paul's combat course in Asia Minor and Macedonia and Achaia would have been more than adequate training for any soldier. He struggled not only through miles and miles of tough mountainous terrain, but also terrors at sea. He kept pushing ahead to the limits of his endurance, all the while suffering from a painful chronic illness that would not let go.

But Paul's commission included a dimension foreign to the marines. He fought not only against flesh and blood, but also against what he called the powers of darkness. Satan marshaled his entire arsenal against Paul, who in the end emerged victorious through Christ's power living in him.

Jesus looks for those willing to be commissioned for spiritual warfare. No higher cause exists in heaven and on earth. Volunteers are needed for his army.

His Evangelistic Motivation

Romans 1:8–17

Jesus issued general instructions to Paul, without the details. "Go," Jesus commanded. "I will send you far away to the Gentiles" (Acts 22:21). At his trial Paul testified to King Agrippa that Jesus had told him, "I am sending you to them [the Gentiles] to open their eyes and turn them from darkness to light . . ." (Acts 26:17–18).

Paul responded obediently to Jesus' orders, but what else caused him to become such a passionate evangelist? Why was he so determined to attack Rome, the very heart and citadel of pagan religion and civilization? What chance did Jesus have against the overwhelming powers of Rome?

Paul explained to the Romans that a profound theological logic compelled him to come to their city. He would come to discharge a debt he owed the pagans. What did he owe them? The good news about Jesus. He had been entrusted with the gospel, which he considered a treasure, and he was accountable for how he administered it (2 Cor 4:7; 2 Tim 1:14).

We stumble over Paul's logic because it is so foreign to our ways of thinking about unbelievers. Generally speaking, we compare the gospel to something like a tip we leave for good service, not a debt to be discharged. If everything falls into place, there are no embarrassing obstacles, and we like the people, we think about inviting them to Jesus if we feel like it.

The waters of Paul's evangelistic eagerness sprang from a different well. The gospel did not embarrass him because it represented God's saving power for everyone who believes. The gospel reveals God's way to forgiveness and eternal life.

God's righteousness is the preeminent issue. God's character outranks everything else in motivating power. If we long to see his righteousness displayed in the world, we will take his message of love and forgiveness without fear of ridicule and shame. Whatever Rome represents to us, it will look like a piece of cake. Rome was supremely powerful in Paul's day, but eventually it succumbed to Jesus.

Paul's eagerness to evangelize can be traced to both discharging a debt and a desire to see God's righteousness at work. He did not limit the scope of his work. He was "obligated both to Greeks and non-Greeks, both to the wise and the foolish" (Rom 1:14). Or, as we might say, to the educated and the uneducated.

Obligated, eager, unashamed. Taken together, for Paul at least, this is what drove him to Rome, where he ultimately perished. Psychologically, he approached his task with a winner's attitude. He boldly told the believers at Rome that he was expecting "a harvest" in their city. Not just one or two converts, but a truckload.

Optimism in the face of huge roadblocks has inspired and motivated evangelists, missionaries, pastors, and teachers, as well as determined Christians in their communities and workplaces. How refreshingly powerful it is to worship in a congregation that seizes evangelistic opportunities despite the difficulties. Paul's example at Rome points the way to success, which begins with proper theology, not slick methods.

Unashamed of the Gospel

Romans 1:16–32

Setting foot on a university campus for the first time I could think of many reasons to be ashamed of the gospel. Was I intellectually adequate? Would what I have to say survive the crucible of unbelief? Christians were a distinct minority, battling against the tides of so-called superior, sophisticated knowledge. Supposedly, science had proved the Bible wrong and critics had savaged the sacred text. Yet my Bible was the only weapon I had and the gospel was the heart of my faith and message.

Perhaps Paul felt something like that when he launched his evangelistic campaign against Rome, the citadel of pagan political and religious power. He had been despised and rejected by the wise men of Athens. How would imperial Rome respond to a message about a crucified, risen savior who claimed to be Lord of the universe? Rome did not take kindly to competing deities.

Paul knew it would be a struggle of power against power. He boldly asserted his faith in God's power, arguing not on the basis of military, political, or philosophical power, but on the basis of theology. Obviously, Rome tightly controlled everything in the visible material world. Paul arrived in Rome with a totally different kind of power, the power to change people's lives and make them fit for eternal life in heaven.

God's power towered over Rome's power because it brought salvation to Jews and Gentiles alike and because it revealed God's way to righteousness. Rome's power existed in an entirely different realm. Rome was powerless to bring people salvation and righteousness. The gospel's power changed the inner person, even though the outer person might be a slave to Rome. Rome could never produce anything comparable.

Paul engaged Rome in the realm of the spirit, the realm of what really makes people tick. He attacked Rome where it was most vulnerable, not its religion, philosophy, and military might, but its moral corruption and degradation. His description reads like it came from a satellite spy plane. He spelled out Rome's root problem—changing God's truth into a lie—and its resulting consequences. An incredibly powerful sickness had engulfed this great city, which lay in the path of God's fearful judgment.

Could the gospel really change Rome? No great revival swept Rome upon Paul's arrival, but in the end Paul's gospel turned the Roman Empire upside down. Jesus became Lord across the Mediterranean world and his church survived long after Rome's power disappeared.

With the growth and establishment of the church came a clear call for people not only to change their allegiance from pagan gods to Jesus, but also to clean up their lives. By accepting rather than suppressing God's truth people could not only gain salvation in heaven, they could also be liberated from the terrible sins Paul cited in his letter to Rome.

Every culture in every generation needs a fresh dose of God's power. Christians can be as strong as Paul was in affirming the gospel's superiority to anything the unbelieving world has to offer. We fail our society if we fail to address its social and spiritual needs with the gospel of God's saving, transforming power.

Of course, our knees knock when we assault strongholds of unbelief, where God's truth is ridiculed and suppressed. But Jesus living in us overcomes our weakness and gives us faith and courage to address people with God's good news in Christ.

Imagine, then, the excited anticipation of the believers in Rome. Paul was coming to reap a harvest among them in their totally defiled and perverted city. Paul would arrive energized with God's power in the gospel of Christ. Surely they would be energized as well, as we should be. They did not have a clue that when he did arrive, it would be in chains. But God's power prevailed nevertheless. In his letter, Paul moved on to the theological foundation of his message.

CHAPTER 11

Theological Groundwork

Having revealed his plans to the Christians at Rome, Paul next expounded the theological heartbeat of his faith. As we mine these rich texts, we want to keep Paul himself in mind, so that we understand theology not just as an academic discipline but as a life-changing force. Creed married conduct in Paul's mind. As we consider the Christian concept of justification before a holy, righteous God, we also want to see the difference it made in Paul's life.

JUSTIFYING JUSTIFICATION

Romans 3:1–31

My discussion with a Jewish friend about our approaches to God seemed to be going nowhere when I asked him how a person gets right with God. "Do you know God's way to become acceptable to him?" I asked. He looked puzzled and I explained that it was through faith in Jesus.

Turning to Romans 3, I showed him that both his Jewish law and prophets pointed to Jesus. In fact, no one can be righteous in God's sight by keeping the law. Trying to please God that way is fruitless. We just can't make it on our own.

Following God's way to righteousness and acceptance means a 100 percent repudiation of working to be good enough to satisfy his holiness and justice. The apostle Paul arrived at this revolutionary truth not by logic but by a personal encounter with Jesus himself. When he met Jesus, Paul's superb righteousness according to the law melted like an ice cream cone in July heat.

The Imitation of Saint Paul

He wrestled with the apparent contradiction. If law-keeping didn't fit him for God, what did? He found the answer in what he called justification, which became the heart of his gospel preaching.

Our efforts to understand this term sometimes resemble the old picnic game of trying to catch a greased pig. Paul didn't tell us how he developed his idea. Perhaps God explained it to him when he was alone with him in the Arabian dessert. At any rate, he discovered God's way to overcome the impenetrable sin barrier between him and God. If his strict, fierce adherence to the law couldn't do it, what could?

Paul could not make himself righteous; God had to do it. That's what he called justification—God's way out of the dilemma posed by his sin and God's holiness and justice. Paul's understanding encompasses the basic problem of our human experience. Everyone has sinned and fallen dismally short of God's holiness and glory. On the other hand, Paul declared, everyone can be made righteous (justified) in God's sight by God's free grace in Jesus Christ.

How did Paul justify God's apparent violation of his own holiness? By pointing to Jesus. How does one banish the terrible blot of sin and its eternal consequences? In God's economy, only by understanding what Jesus did on the cross. In God's plan to save us, he sent Jesus, by whose death our sins are atoned for and the judgment we deserve is blotted out. We are set free from the death we deserve because Jesus died in our place. Therefore, God is at liberty, so to speak, to accept us and make us righteous (justify us).

The cross demonstrates God's justice. The cross proves that God is both himself just and the justifier of anyone who puts his faith in Christ. God has done his part in this equation. Our part is faith. We have to receive, as Paul did, God's grace in his Son.

Chaplain George Rentz received the Navy Cross posthumously for valor in the early World War II Battle of Sunda Strait off Java. After the sinking of the cruiser USS *Houston*, Chaplain Rentz and other sailors clung to any piece of wreckage they could find. After drifting many hours, the chaplain offered his life vest to wounded sailors. At first no one accepted it, but then Seaman First Class Walter Beeson reluctantly took it. He was saved and the chaplain slipped away into the water.

Paul offers us Jesus, the one who died to save us. We perish if we do not accept his life vest.

Abraham's Pivotal Role

Romans 4:1–25

When Paul argued for Jesus, he gave Abraham a pivotal role. He carefully crafted his definition of salvation and acceptance by God according to Abraham's life and witness. He revolutionized Jewish thought by insisting that Abraham's legitimate offspring were those who had confessed Jesus as lord and savior, not those who were descended from his physical line.

Of course, such outrageous thinking earned Paul the undying enmity of the Jews. He was undermining the foundation of their religion and therefore they considered him to be quite dangerous and ultimately worthy of the death sentence. Despite their threats, Paul attacked the law-keeping theology and practice of the Jews frontally without wavering.

By interpreting Abraham as he did, Paul gained the opprobrium "traitor." In his defense, Paul touted himself as the most rigorous devotee of the law. No one could outdo him in terms of religious zeal for the Old Testament laws. But after meeting Jesus, Paul reconsidered his basic values and those he had once held dear he rejected as so much garbage.

In effect, Jesus drove Paul to Abraham, because he was the prototype of all those who would gain salvation and God's righteousness by faith, not by works of the law. Such a mind-boggling approach to God brought Paul on a collision course with the Jews. It also set him apart from the world's religions, all of which promoted some kind of holy living as the key to eternal salvation.

Looking at Abraham's experience with God, Paul grasped the doctrine of God's grace. By faith Abraham had been saved because God's way of righteousness springs from his grace. Grace separates Christian faith from the rest.

Abraham was a formidable leader, well worth the accolade "Israel's father." When he believed God, he was considered righteous by God. Therefore, Paul argued, faith opens the door to our acceptance by God, not our so-called good works.

To drive home his point quite forcefully, Paul reminded the Jews that God had accepted Abraham even before he was circumcised. Of course, circumcision was what made a Jew a Jew. Logically, to the Jews' way of thinking, this rite guaranteed the salvation of Abraham's physical children. Hearing how Paul interpreted Abraham on this crucial point poured gasoline on their fire.

Paul looked beyond the Jews to his Gentile audience. What glorious news he brought them by looking to Abraham. The Gentiles did not have to conform to Jewish rites to be saved. In fact, they inherited God's promises as much as the Jews did. Righteousness comes by faith to Jews and Gentiles alike.

Of course Gentiles of all stripes shared a host of religiously inspired duties, so Abraham's story interpreted by Paul liberated them from their bondage and fear as well. Abraham was the key illustration to bringing people together under Christ's lordship. Abraham believed God's promises. Christians believe in the supreme promise of the ages—God credits righteousness to those who believe in the crucified, resurrected Jesus.

Although Abraham sometimes failed and took matters into his own hands, he stands as the prime example of one who persevered in faith. So we cling to Jesus while we face various struggles of our own.

Paul's bedrock lesson from Abraham is that we do not need to be good enough to gain God's pleasure. Because we live in union with Jesus, God looks on us as totally acceptable. In Christ he grants us eternal right standing before him.

Paul's desire was that his theology would move from head to heart, that Christian conduct would issue from Christian creed. We do well to follow his example: study to understand theology and determine to live like people accepted and justified by God.

We use Paul as the model of our faith; he used Abraham to prove that our salvation depends on God's grace alone. Coming up, we examine Paul's personal battle and struggle in his own soul.

CHAPTER 12

Path to Victory

Paul's path to victory was not a cakewalk. Far from it. He had found God's recipe for his own spiritual growth and he basked in God's deliverance from sin's penalty and power. At the same time, a tumultuous storm raged within his soul. His honesty stirs us to follow his example and flee to Christ.

Recipe for Growth

Romans 5:1–11

Recipe publishers follow a standard format: first, list all the needed ingredients; second, print step-by-step instructions to make the finished product. Paul's recipe for spiritual growth looks something like that. That this was Paul's personal recipe is clear because he included himself in "we." The first person singular "I" would fit just as well. Since our goal is to imitate him, we must carefully follow his recipe.

Paul's recipe for spiritual growth begins with the essential ingredient he called justification. Earlier in his letter to the Romans, he described in considerable detail what justification looked and tasted like. He said it was God's way of making unrighteous, unholy people righteous and holy. To make it work, said Paul, you have to follow Abraham's faith example. In Paul's doctrine, God's way succeeded because Jesus Christ died to satisfy God's justice and holiness.

Paul's faith in God's justification through Jesus gave him peace, delivered him from onerous law-keeping, and moved him into the house of

God's grace. To make bread, you start with yeast and after dry yeast works for awhile in hot water, you add flour to produce living dough. In Paul's recipe, faith is like the power of yeast. It transformed him so thoroughly that he rejoiced in the prospect of future glory.

Every bread recipe varies according to the baker's pleasure. You can make standard white bread, whole wheat bread, French bread, sourdough bread, and so on. Paul's unique recipe included something that looks and tastes foul to us: suffering. We do not willingly choose to throw suffering into the mix of our lives.

However, Paul went beyond accepting suffering as a necessary ingredient. He claimed he was happy about it. Why? Because as a spiritual cook, so to speak, he knew the end product. Often, when I try a new recipe, even after I scrupulously follow the instructions, I'm not sure what it will taste like. Not so with Paul.

He rejoiced, he said, because his bread tasted much better with a cup of suffering. Suffering trained him to endure. Endurance proved that he had character, that he had stood the test of his faith.

Remember how relieved you were when you passed a critical exam in school. That grade gave you hope that you might graduate after all. Paul felt the same way. He passed, as it were, and was overcome with genuine—not phony—joy.

I like my hot fudge sundaes dripping with dark swirls of thick sauce laced with peanuts. Whatever you think of as the icing on the cake of your favorite dessert, in Paul's testimony about his life in God's grace through Christ he cited the flood of God's love.

To be absolutely certain of God's unfailing love, Paul continually looked to Jesus on the cross. His dying savior propelled him not just to endure suffering, but to rejoice in it. Jesus constituted the centerpiece of Paul's recipe for growth.

Sometimes I try a new recipe and after dinner we vote on whether or not it is a keeper. From time to time the world offers new recipes for spiritual growth. No matter how appealing they look, they are not keepers because they do not make Jesus the centerpiece. As we follow Paul, he consistently leads us to his lord and savior Jesus Christ.

From Slavery to Freedom to Slavery

Romans 6:1–23

People who witness the liftoff of a spacecraft at Cape Canaveral stand spellbound at the brilliant, awesome power generated by the rockets at ground zero. Even those who watch from fifty miles away sense the explosive energy required to boost the vessel into space. Once free of gravity, however, the astronauts on board are released to carry out their duties.

In his earthbound existence, Paul sensed a similar feeling of power over a force that is every bit as intractable as gravity—the grip of sin, which he called slavery. He had been freed from captivity to the law when he discovered Jesus. He found that God's way to righteousness was not by rigidly adhering to rules, but by confessing faith in Jesus.

But such freedom was fraught with peril. Paul considered the possibility that prisoners freed from the law might rush headlong into destructive behavior. With no restraints, the sky was the limit.

Therefore, Paul rushed to plug the gap, not with a new set of rules but with a radical dynamic—the indwelling life of Jesus Christ. Paul massaged in his own mind over and over the basics of what God had done for him in Christ. He recalled historical facts about Jesus: his death, burial, and resurrection. These constituted the cornerstone of both his salvation and his ensuing Christian experience.

Just as if he had been a passenger on a US space mission, Paul hitched himself totally to what Jesus had done for him. Everything depended on Jesus. When Jesus died, Paul died; when Jesus was buried, Paul was buried; when Jesus was raised, Paul was raised. Voila! He escaped his slavery to sin.

Looking at these facts, Paul realized it was nonsense to go on sinning. Since he was free from sin's downward pull, he was also free to live for a new master. Everything he had and did, as a result, could be dedicated to God. What God had done for him in Christ determined how he would use his mind, heart, will, and body.

In fact, Paul discovered that, because sin's power had been thwarted by Jesus and he had been turned loose, he could enter an entirely new and different kind of slavery. He became a slave to good living. Immorality's power was eternally broken so that morality and righteousness might rule in its place.

Paul attributed his radical transformation to God's grace. His freedom from sin and enslavement to righteousness had nothing to do with his own efforts to please God. Everything was a gift from the God of all grace.

We know the source of the power at Cape Canaveral's blastoffs. Paul knew that God's grace empowered his life. Such power transcends all of man's capabilities in terms of rocket launches. While it takes hundreds of pages of physics to describe what happens at blastoff, Paul reduced his spiritual physics and chemistry to one simple sentence: "But now that you have been set free from sin and have becomes slaves to God, the benefit you reap leads to holiness, and the result is eternal life" (Rom 6:22).

Paul's heart thumped as he released the shattering news to the world. He reduced life to its essence and broke the shackles of sin's slavery to give us freedom to enlist as slaves to Jesus instead.

FIGHTINGS WITHIN

Romans 7:1–25

Probably in no other experience does Paul draw us so intensely into such painful identity with himself than in the conflict that raged in his soul. "Paul," we confess, "we know exactly what you are talking about. Too often we do things we don't want to do, and we don't do what we know we should do."

In one sense, perhaps, we find a measure of comfort. We reason, "If the great apostle had his problems with sin, certainly I must not be in such bad shape." However, such thinking must never excuse behaviors that break our fellowship with God.

Our brief meditation does not attempt to resolve different interpretations of Romans 7. Our goal is to get inside Paul the best we can and focus on the big picture. To begin, we cannot help but thank God for the brutal honesty with which Paul addressed his problem. Why did he risk airing his own wars with sin? Why admit to the new believers in Rome that they were headed for continual battles with sin?

Because it was the truth and even Paul was not immune to the powerful pulls of his old sin nature. Paul did not attempt a psychological rationale, nor did he try to paper over his own flaws. Rather, he was honest, candid and vulnerable. He looked into his own heart and will and decided that the best possible way to teach new believers was to expose his inner turmoil to them. Surely, there is much we can learn from him in a culture that ranks self-image and reputation above spiritual values of humility and integrity.

Confession of failures rarely break out in Christian relationships and communities. Who wants to admit, "I'm having a battle with . . .?" Yet such transparency seems to be an important way to illuminate spiritual reality and to claim Christ's indwelling power.

To get inside Paul, as it were, requires terribly painful honesty about sin's grip on us. Perhaps such pain is difficult to take in the twenty-first century because sin has lost its grip on our culture's conscience. We just don't hear or read about it much anymore. Some terrible crime occurs and explanations and excuses are devoid of the recognition of sin. Not so with Paul. He knew precisely where to look for his troubles.

The first crucial step to success and healing is confession. The second? Find the key to deliverance in Jesus Christ. "Who is there to rescue me?" cried Paul. "God alone, through Jesus Christ our Lord!" (Rom 7:24–25, NEB).

Suddenly, this "miserable creature" (Rom 7:24, NEB) became a confident, triumphant Christian. Such must be every believer's passion. Paul searched everywhere within himself and he found no solutions, even in his super-righteous religious upbringing, his marvelous education, and his zealous pursuit of those people in Jerusalem he perceived to be God's enemies. He came up totally empty until he turned to Jesus.

Paul's deeply cherished ambition was to "present everyone perfect in Christ" (Col 1:28). To accomplish that goal, he bared his soul, so that we might discover daily rescues from sin, as it were, through our thirst for Jesus and his satisfying life.

We wrestle with Paul's story and try to make everything fit. We like to have neat, predigested answers. We try the Pop-Tart approach and it doesn't work that way. Some things just don't fit. How could Paul be dead to sin and yet confess his failures? I don't know for sure, but I thank God he delivers me when I confess and ask Jesus to clean up my act.

Next, we look at Paul's supreme confidence and his indomitable faith.

CHAPTER 13

The Summit of His Faith

Christians who go to their Bibles for confidence and assurance of God's love most assuredly turn to Paul's summit of faith in Romans 8. Here we find him considering the worst of all possible outcomes. And yet, infused with the Holy Spirit, he marches triumphantly to a most satisfying conclusion.

SUPREME CONFIDENCE

Romans 8:28–30

Helping people to get their stories into print has brought me uncountable treasures. One of the most satisfying came from God's giving me a friendship with a retired missionary, Eva Mills. Eva lived in the same Lancaster, Pennsylvania, retirement home that my mother did, so our paths crossed early on. The first time I met her I recognized pure gold, refined after serving Jesus fifty years in Brazil.

Regardless of her incurable illness, her eyes sparkled and her smile charmed me. I could not say No when she asked me to edit her book, which told the story of her life in Brazil. She called it "8:28."

Eva had landed in Brazil August 8, 1928. More importantly, her life powerfully testified to the truth of Paul's superb affirmation of his confidence in God's good and perfect will. Virtually every day, I suspect, countless numbers of Christians recite this verse in the midst of shattering circumstances.

The Summit of His Faith

Simply put, Paul trusted that in the end everything would be all right. All his battles would conclude on the positive side. Nothing fell outside the scope of Paul's possibilities. "All things" meant exactly that.

One of his battles concerned sin in his life (Romans 7). Constantly, his sinful nature engaged the Holy Spirit. He was deeply concerned about the spiritual health and growth of his converts, some of whom had lapsed into terrible sin. He fought against false teachers and defectors. Persecution and hardships of many kinds assaulted him. Paul bagged them in "all things."

Essentially, Paul saw God's hand in everything. God had not spun him off. God had not told him he was on his own while he attended to other matters. Whatever happened, Paul acknowledged God's handiwork.

But did everything add up on the "good" side of his personal ledger? "Yes," Paul would say, "but only if you step back and look at the big picture of what God is doing for those who love him." For Paul, to love meant to trust and obey. For those believers, God has initiated an eternal program (his calling) and the end result will be good.

Paul was not so naïve as to suggest that all of life's experiences feel good. Some of them are bad and they really hurt. Suffering is painful. Our fallen world is victimized by incredible effects of sin. When disaster and tragedy strike, we ask, "God, how can this be for my good?"

Paul's supreme confidence did not lead him to gloss over such things, or to pretend that evil does not exist. Rather, God works according to his pattern for our good, not according to what we think is good for us. Paul kept that pattern foremost in his thinking. It looked like this:

God wants to make us like Jesus, the epitome of perfection. He makes us righteous so we can enjoy his presence. He will glorify us. Put together, Paul thought, there is nothing better. This is superlative, incomparable goodness. It encompasses past, present, and future.

I used to watch my mother make her dresses. It was a crazy scene. She cut the paper. Ouch! She cut the material. Ouch! She sewed it, pressed it, trimmed it, tried it on, stuck pins in it. Ouch, ouch, and ouch! As I considered the pieces lying on the floor, nothing seemed to fit. How could a dress come out of this mess? Suddenly, it all came together and it was good.

"So," Paul said, in effect, "I trust God to take care of all my ouches, piece them together, and in the end make something good."

More than Conquerors

Romans 8:31–39

I sat in a darkened room with an elderly Chinese Christian woman, who had fled China at the height of the communist takeover. An old stone farmhouse in Pennsylvania provided refuge and comfort for her, under the tender ministries of her aging American missionary companion. Together, they fleshed out for me Paul's testimony of overwhelming victory in Christ.

Christiana Tsai suffered from an incurable illness that forced her to wear dark glasses while she was confined to bed in her room where I could barely make out her face and limbs. Somehow, her voice communicated that she had more than defeated ostracism, chronic illness, and the loss of her property, station in life, family, friends, and homeland.

My wife, two children and I clustered around her bed and allowed her to infuse us with the powerful presence of Jesus. Nothing in her life had separated her from God's love in Jesus. Nary a trace of a whimper escaped her lips. The tune she played so vibrantly radiated with contentment and optimism.

In fact, the light of Jesus splashed throughout her room so brilliantly that nationalist Chinese army officers, training at a nearby US Army camp, were drawn to her like moths to a lamp. They met Jesus there and turned to him in trusting, believing faith.

Christiana's story resembled Paul's in many ways. Scholars think he was somewhat debilitated by an incurable illness, perhaps malaria that dimmed his eyesight. But as he looked back at what God had done for him in Christ, he contemplated the unknown, not with fear and anxiety, but with the supreme confidence of a fighter who has disposed of all his foes, past, present, and future.

Perhaps he struggled for the right words to convey his optimism. True, he had conquered all previous attacks on his body, soul, and spirit, but that was not enough for him. Jesus so permeated his life that he had done more than defeat his enemies; he had somehow risen above them.

Paul spoke in superlatives when it came to picturing the deep reservoir of his resources in Christ. God was on his side, proved by Christ's sacrificial death for him. Therefore, the future held more lavish gifts of God's incomparable grace.

The Summit of His Faith

Paul contemplated the worst possibility: judgment at God's hand. No sweat, because Jesus pleads his case before God. Jesus pleads his atoning death and resurrection. Therefore, he secured Paul's eternal destiny.

Paul looked next at the calamities that had befallen him. Where was God in his afflictions, hardships, persecution, hunger, nakedness, and perils to the point of death by the sword? Still showering him with the love of Jesus. Nothing can stanch the thundering falls of Niagara and nothing can thwart the love of Jesus.

Then he raised his pen in a paean of praise, sort of like the climax of Beethoven's *Ninth Symphony*. He considered every possible arena of spiritual and physical battle, now and to the end of time, and concluded that Christ's love would always sustain him.

Thank you, Paul, for showing Christiana Tsai and us how to bring light into the dark rooms of our lives.

His New Mind

Romans 12:1–2

Athletes compete mentally as well as physically. To get even a slight edge in the game, players try to penetrate their opponents' minds with taunts and insults. "He was trying to get inside my head," a player tells reporters after the game. "He was playing mind games with me." The strategy works if a player loses his cool and the game.

Paul's spiritual warfare drew him into some fierce mental battles. He played mind games all the time. Not really games, of course, but life and death struggles. He knew his ultimate opponent, Satan, held people in his grip by blinding their minds. Paul also knew that Christ's great commandment called him to love Jesus with his entire mind.

Therefore, having decided to follow Jesus, Paul discovered his transformed mind. His transformation caused him to think differently about himself, God, the world, Jesus, salvation, and his personal ambitions. Paul tells us that he used to think like a child, but he had put that behind him. "Now I know in part; then I shall know fully," he explained (1 Cor 13:1).

Once he had proudly bragged about his accomplishments. He thought his approach to God was set in concrete, impregnable from any quarter. Self-righteously, he had risen to the challenge of Christianity, fully convinced he was on the right track.

61

However, with his transformed mind he saw things quite differently. So differently, in fact, that he had thrown all of his badges of honor on the garbage dump. His salvation rested not on his zealous adherence to the law, but on Christ's righteousness given to him by faith.

Paul had learned the truth about Jesus. But his was more than an intellectual conversion. Beyond knowing the truth, he sought to live like Jesus. Only the mind of Jesus could replace Paul's proud, self-driven, mistaken mind. He found his model of humility in the mind of Jesus and he pleaded with his converts to open themselves to the mind of Christ.

Like World War I trench warfare in Western Europe, Christ and the devil fought back and forth for control of Paul's mind. Paul emerged victorious because Christ's peace, "which transcends all understanding" (Phil 4:7), guarded his mind. His ultimate defense in his "mind games" with Satan came from his intimate walk with Jesus.

Paul's transformed mind enabled him to replace ungodly, fleshly thoughts with pure thoughts. So all-encompassing was his new mind that he focused on the true and the good, on things that were lovely, gracious, excellent, and admirable. He urged his followers to fill their minds with such things.

Further, Paul kept the devil from getting into his head by concentrating on Jesus and heaven. "Set your minds on things above, not on earthly things," he appealed (Col 3:2). This is certainly possible, he explained, because his mind had been renewed in God's image.

That was possibly the most significant fact Paul revealed about what he called his "new self" (Col 3:10). In effect, he had access to God's mind for wisdom in preaching, for guidance in ministry, and for holiness in living. What he labeled his transformed mind was a mind being continually renewed in God's wisdom and knowledge.

When our minds are remade in God's image, we follow his truth unequivocally and obey his commands for holy living. We are totally transformed and completely fulfilled in our knowledge of his perfectly good and pleasing will.

Paul's renewed mind produced his indomitable faith and hope. Without the mind of Christ, he would have fallen into depression and despair when he thought about what the future might hold for him. To be more than conquerors, we must follow Paul's example here and ask God for daily renewal of our minds to remind us of his overarching love.

Paul experienced and wrote about his patience in times of trouble. Like a football coach on the sidelines, he wanted his readers to charge the goal line with unflagging zeal and energy, because that was what he had done and would continue to do.

Our next step in imitating Paul takes us to his enduring faith and obedience.

CHAPTER 14

Still Marching On

At the conclusion of Paul's Letter to the Romans we find the battered warrior still marching on. Faced with certain troubles ahead, he remained totally dedicated to Christ's mission for him. Nothing deterred him, even at this stage of his life. His example challenges our thinking about our faithful obedience to Christ.

Patient in Tribulation

Romans 12:9–16

I am not a paragon of patience. Waiting in line to pay for my groceries tests my patience. Over the years, however, God has taught me patience in various trials far tougher than the checkout line.

No stranger to tribulation himself, Paul filled his letters with exhortations to patience and he extolled the spiritual power and virtues of patience. He spoke as an eminently qualified counselor, not out of psychological theory. After all, he said, God is the God of patience (Rom 15:5, KJV).

A cursory look at his life shows how God shaped Paul's patience. For example, he waited patiently for a week in Damascus after being blinded by the brilliant light of Jesus that stunned him along his way from Jerusalem. Then when he aspired to teach the Christians he had previously hurt, they rejected him and sent him back to Tarsus where he waited patiently for some sign to begin the mission Jesus had assigned him.

Sometime later, he went off by himself to the desert in Arabia, where he said he had received doctrinal instruction from the Lord. Such an interlude, fascinating as it was, included more than classroom work, as it were. God was building patience in his servant.

Summoned from Tarsus by his friend Barnabas, Paul took up teaching the new church at Antioch. God blessed his work there. However, important as it was, it was a way station en route to his evangelistic mission. He learned to be patient. At last, called by the Holy Spirit, Paul set out with Barnabas on their first teaching mission. Soon tribulation set in. Opposition confronted them everywhere, including stoning. Paul patiently persisted despite many hardships.

Patience in tribulation became his life's pattern. Some tribulation was physical as he endured stoning, flogging, mob attacks, sleeplessness, hunger, shipwreck, and imprisonment. Add to this his emotional and spiritual tribulation: defection of associates, immorality in the church, false teachers, and loneliness. Paul also endured the tribulation of persistent illness. He asked God for relief, but the answer was No. He patiently suffered, drawing on Christ's power for strength in his weakness.

After his arrest in Jerusalem and his appeal to Caesar, Paul waited two years in prison in Caesarea before Festus took up his case. Tribulation followed him en route to Rome when his ship sank. Finally, he arrived in Rome where he was placed under household arrest, awaiting trial.

Perhaps several years elapsed before he was found guilty and condemned to die. Waiting with uncertainty about the outcome of his case placed perhaps the greatest pressure on Paul's patience. He had been given a glimpse of heaven, and he longed to be with Christ. What could be harder to bear than knowing what heaven is like and yet not being able to go there?

Paul's congregations were also under considerable pressure, facing accusations from Jews and pagans alike. They expected that somehow Jesus would return and deliver them from the terrors of Rome. Paul counseled the Thessalonians to wait patiently for Christ. For him, patience was not a matter of glumly bearing tribulation. Rather, he took an aggressive approach and attacked tribulation with patience.

Patience was a powerful antidote to anxiety, fear, suffering, and depression in Paul's mind. Patience helped him not only to endure tribulation, but also to rejoice in it. Jesus was his model and his indwelling source of patience. Our patience enables us to stand firm in trouble, whatever it may be.

Mission Accomplished

Romans 15:14–22

Critics of the war in Iraq seized on a banner, "Mission Accomplished," displayed on the *USS Abraham Lincoln*, to ridicule former President George W. Bush's televised speech from the carrier's deck on May 1, 2003, highlighting the end of major combat operations. Of course, in hindsight we understand the banner's declaration was premature. The battle raged for years after that.

Paul made a similar announcement to the church at Rome. Trying to explain why he had not visited the Christians there, he gave a brief resume of what he had been doing. Short as it was, it was nonetheless staggering in its scope and import.

He explained what his goal had been: to preach the gospel to the Gentiles, especially where people did not know Jesus Christ. In his quest to fulfill his mission he had traveled from Jerusalem to Illyricum; that is, from the eastern provinces of the Roman Empire to the province of Illyricum on the east coast of the Adriatic Sea.

Amazingly, in a comparatively short time frame, Paul had evangelized roughly half of the Roman world. Of course, he did not preach in every single hamlet and village. He did not follow every trail into the mountains and down to the sea. Instead, he concentrated on the major metropolitan areas. From there the Jesus story spread widely (Col 1:6; 1 Thess 1:8).

He never claimed to have done it all by himself. Not only did Christians spread the Jesus story; other evangelists were also at work. But Paul went to great pains to explain that he (and his companions) worked in virgin territories where others had not yet gone with the gospel.

Paul gave credit to Jesus and to the Holy Spirit for the accomplishment of his mission. He downplayed the human element in the story, so that Jesus might receive the glory. Because he was Christ's obedient servant, he could say that Jesus had worked through him.

The Holy Spirit had wrought signs and miracles to break down barriers and to open the door to faith among the pagans. Luke's record in the Book of Acts includes examples of how this paved the way for Paul's preaching.

Far from Paul's mind was any notion of personal accomplishment. He saw his work not as a chance to accumulate laurels for himself, but to make an offering to God. He himself served as a living sacrifice and he presented his converts as an offering to God. In his understanding he was just fulfilling the purpose for which God had called him. His evangelism constituted the "good works" God had ordained for him (Eph 2:10).

Being so voluntarily committed to Jesus, Paul escaped the bondage of earning his way to God's good pleasure. He was liberated from preaching as a burden and a chore. His mission did not drag him down, but rather it inspired him to press on to unevangelized regions. What he called his "priestly duty" kept him on target. His sense of duty filtered through to the new Christians who came to share his passion for evangelism.

In Paul's dispensation he accomplished God's mission and the church was successfully launched. However, he gave no hints that the fight for gospel truth was over. Others followed in his footsteps to bring the church to where it is today. Church history ebbs and flows with victories and defeats. But God gives every Christian the duty to declare "mission accomplished" in obedience to his will and for the advance of the gospel.

On to Spain

Romans 15:17–29

At one time I believed I was going to do missionary work in Latin America, but God had other plans for me. Rather than do mission work on the field, I became a journalist and editor for the cause of worldwide missions. Similarly, Paul had his heart set on taking the gospel to Spain, but he never got there.

As far as Paul was concerned, there was no stopping him from doing what Jesus had told him to do: "I am sending you to them to open their eyes and turn them from darkness to light . . . so that they may receive forgiveness of sins . . . So then, King Agrippa, I was not disobedient to the vision from heaven" (Acts 26:18–19). Consequently, he had preached from Jerusalem to Turkey to Greece to Serbia.

He was determined to take Jesus to places where no one else had gone with the good news, including Rome, the citadel of idolatrous emperor worship. He would stop over in Rome on his way to Spain. He envisioned a great harvest in Rome and beyond.

Paul knew the perils awaiting him in Jerusalem. Eventually he arrived in Rome, not as a free man but as a prisoner. He never made it to Spain. But "on to Spain" could very well serve as a concluding epitaph to his remarkable career.

Here was a person who could have legitimately signed off the dreadful pressures he endured as a traveling evangelist. What could have motivated him to keep going? Primarily, of course, he kept going because Spain represented another part of the world where the gospel must be preached. He saw no limits to his work as long as he had physical strength and the means to travel.

Paul did not see evangelism as a career from which one could earn retirement. His was a lifetime calling because Jesus was Lord and he gave the orders. Doubtless, Paul had heard from the Holy Spirit many times, telling him where to go. He did not pick Spain on a personal whim.

If Rome and Spain were so crucial in his thinking, we might well ask why Paul chose to go to Jerusalem knowing that he might be arrested. Along the way Christians had tried to deter him, but he went in spite of their warnings. In the end, he appealed his case to Caesar and thus he did find his way to Rome.

Paul's "on to Spain" spirit is the same spirit that has driven countless missionaries to set similar goals for themselves. They have spent years researching the people of the world, trying to identify those who have never heard the gospel. Many have given their lives in martyrdom for the sake of bringing Jesus to hostile tribes.

Paul's relentless pursuit of new territory to evangelize pictures a person so committed to Christ that the thought of quitting apparently never occurred to him. His letters emphasize what it cost him to persevere in his calling. Yet he never saw himself as an empire builder. The results of his mission followed his passion to know Christ and to be found in him.

Following Paul's model demands wisdom, sacrifice and perhaps a radical change in one's life goals and priorities. For example, a young woman in her late twenties with a solid career decided to visit an orphanage in Uganda. She fell in love with the children and the staff, resigned her position, and returned to work fulltime at the orphanage. As we pray and follow Jesus, he shows us the role he wants us to play in taking Jesus "on to Spain."

Paul marched on, as it were, even under household arrest. His spirit never flagged. To imitate him, we must continually seek God's will and direction for whatever "Spain" may represent for us. At the same time, we honestly represent Jesus to those around us, who watch us in our households, offices, and playgrounds.

We move on from Romans to First Corinthians and look first at how Paul characterized his role in starting the church at Corinth.

CHAPTER 15

Preacher, Farmer, and Builder

Paul knew a lot more about the Corinthians than he did about the Romans. His First Letter to the Corinthians covers the harsh realities of both church life and his personal ministry. After telling the Corinthians about his deep concerns about cliques in their church, he backtracked, as it were, and revealed his own roles in their spiritual birth: preacher, farmer and builder.

THE NERVOUS, SHAKING PREACHER

1 Corinthians 2:1–10

One day our youth pastor, who preaches occasionally, asked me if I still get nervous when I preach. I assured him that I did, even though I have been preaching off and on for more than sixty years. You realize that even with good preparation and prayer, there's always the chance you will stumble over a word or say something irrelevant that pops into your head from out of nowhere.

Because preaching is empowered by the Holy Spirit it is also subject to the devil's attacks. One of America's truly great twentieth-century preachers, Harold John Ockenga of Boston's Park Street Church, once told me that the devil always seemed to attack him in the pulpit when he got to the climax of the gospel story. Satan likes nothing better than to have the gospel garbled, or soft-pedaled from the pulpit.

Nevertheless, we confess surprise when we read Paul's confession of nervousness when he spoke the gospel at Corinth. On the other hand, it makes me feel better, knowing that the great apostle also got the shakes in front of people. I can identify with that.

But Paul's confession also illuminates some other significant facts about himself and his role as a pioneer evangelist in pagan territory. The first is that he saw himself engaged in a battle for the hearts and minds of the Corinthians. Academic debaters vied for audiences in ancient Greek and Roman culture. Debates provided entertainment, perhaps something like wrestling matches.

Paul, however, entered the arena and joined the fray not to win a debate with a display of fine words and wisdom. Life and death truth gripped him. Eternal destinies hung in the balance. God's wisdom and God's truth challenged the popular ideas of the day. Truth really mattered, not for intellectual satisfaction but for the souls of women and men.

Paul was a scared preacher because he propounded a simple, clear idea that blew away anything the Greeks had to offer: the man Jesus Christ of Nazareth in Galilee (a Roman province) had been nailed to a cross in Jerusalem and rose from the dead, so that anyone—Jew or Greek—might find eternal salvation in him. Christ's crucifixion loomed as the crucial, distinctive component of Paul's speeches.

He shook when he preached, lest he somehow neglected to make the cross clear as finely polished silver, and also because he knew how the Greeks and Jews despised the cross. The idea of God sending his Son to die repelled them and they might run Paul out of town, as had happened elsewhere.

Paul's nerves were on edge also because he feared that he might win some converts attracted by his smooth words and clever arguments. Two passions controlled him: make the gospel clear and be sure his converts' faith responds to God's power and not his words. Speaking with conviction by spiritual power was his prime concern.

His preaching brought both internal and external pressures: physical abuses as well as emotional strains. Yet Paul never wavered from his commission. Nervous he might well be, but he never backed off from a chance to tell people about Jesus. As long as Jesus was the issue, Paul conquered his fears. He may have shook inside when he preached at Corinth, but God did a mighty work through him.

God strengthens and emboldens weak, fearful, shaking Christians who make Jesus the centerpiece of their lives and witness.

The Farmer

1 Corinthians 3:1–9

I spent my childhood on a farm and I learned the basics of farming, but—to my father's disappointment—I never threw myself into it like he did. He was totally committed, while I stood on the periphery and did what I was told to do. However, many, many years later I redeemed myself in his eyes when I became a suburban homeowner and decided to plant a garden.

Since then, during the winter's doldrums, I can hardly wait until spring comes. I buy vegetable seeds, draw my garden plans on paper, work the soil and tenderly deposit those tiny seeds with a loving hand pat. And every year we savor bountiful harvests.

Jesus talked about spreading his kingdom like that. Paul picked up on his analogy. The city of Corinth, and other places he visited, loomed before him like a gigantic farm that potentially would produce a harvest of believers and become a living organism, the church.

In God's kingdom economy, Paul was Christ's hired hand. "I'm just a servant," he said repeatedly. In his vision of the kingdom he didn't own the land. He never saw himself as lord of the manor telling people what to do.

Paul got his hands dirty. He worked with calluses and crusty finger nails. He perspired and agonized over his seeds (the gospel of Christ). He nourished and prayed over those seeds as part of God's team, which included other workers who watered the soil.

Corinth was tough but Paul's seeds prevailed. The church sprouted and grew. The tender shoots endured hard days. The church was born. As Jesus had predicted, the field was ripe for harvest.

I have old black and white photos of my dad proudly standing at the end of a corn row, holding some huge, golden ears. He was not a braggart, but he liked to show off his corn. If I had asked him, he would have given God the credit, for he knew that in the end, despite his weeks and weeks of hard work, he never made the corn grow, but God did.

The Builder

1 Corinthians 3:9–15

My neighbor down the street decided to remodel and enlarge his house. As his work progressed in fits and starts, we wondered if he had bitten off more than he could chew. Workers came and went and then stopped altogether. The project languished for months. Meanwhile, his family struggled to find normalcy in the midst of chaos.

Occasionally, some of our churches resemble this remodeling project—not the actual building structure, but the internal structure of life and faith. When Paul looked at the church at Corinth, he was not pleased with what he saw. Serious flaws abounded, threatening the church's unity, growth, and witness.

The foundation was secure. Like a skilled master builder, Paul himself had laid it. Jesus Christ anchored the church. Jesus provided security and stability. He gave his life for the church, he rose again to indwell the church, and he sent his Holy Spirit to guide the church. What a solid, unshakable foundation we have in him!

Paul's skill shone through when he first arrived at Corinth, determined "to know nothing while I was with you except Jesus Christ and him crucified" (1 Cor 2:2). He constructed the church's spiritual foundation with God's power, not with human wisdom and cleverness. Christ nailed to the cross constituted the cornerstone, even though this was foolishness to the Greeks and a stumbling block to the Jews.

Paradoxically, from a purely human standpoint, Paul's foundation appeared faulty to the world. What building materials did Paul use? Few of his building blocks were influential people. The unbelieving society thought his church was comprised of weak, foolish, contemptible people—mere nothings (1 Cor 1:26–29).

The wise master-builder seized the essence of the gospel and the spirit of Christ's kingdom. These weak, contemptible people demonstrated God's wisdom, righteousness, holiness, and redemption. How could any spiritual contractor improve on that?

But Paul the superlative contractor worried about how his structure fared under successive builders. He clearly categorized their work by the materials they used: gold, silver, costly stones on the one hand, or wood, hay, or straw on the other. Obviously, the first group pleased him, but not the second, made up of perishable materials susceptible to fire. He looked far down the road to God's judgment. Tragically, what started well could end in disaster, even with a perfect foundation.

Paul's portrayal of himself as a master-builder and the church as the building helps us to understand the critical importance of both the foundation and the super-structure. Apart from Jesus, the church stands no chance of survival. Apart from the cross, there is no foundation.

At the same time, each generation of builders risks using shoddy, flammable materials and these builders face severe judgment because God takes his building—the church—very seriously. Anyone who destroys God's temple will be destroyed in the end.

Such was Paul's stance at Corinth, where some people were bragging about different gospel "farmers." Paul would have none of that. He never took credit for the harvests, which were the result of the Holy Spirit's mysterious, unseen work in the hearts and lives of women and men.

In effect, Paul said something like: "I'm not trying to get a personal following. After all, I came here simply as God's servant and all I did was plant the seed and lay the foundation. To God be all the glory and praise for the harvest."

He also acknowledged the value and importance of his fellow workers. They had watered the seed. Regardless of how good your seed is, without water and sun there will be no fruit. In God's fields, all the workers deserve equal credit for the good food.

How gracious and self-effacing Paul was. He simply had carried out the task assigned to him by God. Paul's self-image did not need to be puffed up with success. There was satisfaction enough in doing what he was supposed to do. After all, Jesus had said that even when you've done everything demanded of you, you are still an unworthy servant (Luke 17:10).

All Christians are God's farm hands and builders, as it were, and each one can joyfully and obediently play his or her vital role in God's harvest and building.

It's hard to miss the impact of Paul's imagery. Following his pattern will be costly, involving countless risks and commanding the best of our time and energy. Loving God with our hearts, souls, minds, and strength makes us successful farmers and builders in God's kingdom.

Paul does not show himself to us in a systematic way, so we have to pull together his personal references from various parts of his letters. The next chapter considers from several different angles a major theme in his life: his accountability to God.

CHAPTER 16

Accountable Passion

Passion risks running amok if it is not guarded by accountability. Paul pictured himself both as God's steward and father of the church at Corinth. Accountability guarded his work, which was dominated by his passion to take the gospel through what he called "open doors."

Accountable to God

1 Corinthians 3:12–14; 4:4; 2 Corinthians 5:10; Romans 14:10–12

When my teenage son expressed some resistance to some of my family rules, I decided it was time for a little chat. "John," I said, "you may think some of my rules are unreasonable, but let me explain where I'm coming from. God has committed you to my care and one day I am going to have to answer to him for how well I did or did not perform my duty."

He looked at me with noticeable shock. "Really?" he asked. "Absolutely," I said. "I am accountable to him for how I bring you up. I want to be sure I do a good job."

"I never saw it that way," he said as his resistance melted.

Paul wanted to be sure his converts knew he was accountable to God. God's judgment is coming, both universally and personally. "The Lord judges me" was stamped on Paul's soul like the brand on a calf's hide.

Judgment was not a new idea, of course. The ancient Jews left records of what it cost them when they disobeyed God. New Testament believers considered those stories to be like railroad crossing bells, lights and gates. Israel suffered painful lessons for disobedience. Paul knew those stories well and he prepared himself for judgment.

Accountable Passion

But we never get the idea that Paul was scared. Accountable? Yes. Frightened? No. He reveled in God's forgiving grace and the absolute assurance that no condemnation awaited him. God's righteousness fell upon him when he confessed Jesus as lord.

Yet he knew accountability to God as a wholesome, edifying experience. For one thing, it delivered him from wasting time worrying about what other people thought about him. Who cares about human judges when you have an Almighty Judge in heaven?

Accountability to God drove Paul to strive for excellence in all he did. He could not conceive of using wood, hay and straw in building something for God. He knew that God's judgment fires would expose the quality of his workmanship.

Paul firmly believed that God's judgment seat awaited him. This was perhaps the healthiest aspect of accountability. He foresaw cosmic consequences for what he did in his time on earth, neatly dividing everything into good and bad. Not for him were so-called gray areas. Paul did not equivocate or look for extenuating circumstances. He knew that whatever excuses he might bring would dissolve like butter in a hot skillet before God's unerring, righteousness judgment.

Accountability to God also spared Paul from the nonsense and futility of judging others. He knew the wasteful pain of trying to be judge and jury. God's judgment seat is the only one that counts.

Of course, Paul made value judgments about Christian conduct. Unerringly, fearlessly he told Christians how to behave, what to do and what not to do, so that all of life would fall under Christ's lordship. That was the whole point of accountability. God would hold him accountable according to his righteous standards.

In the hopeless welter of a Roman and Greek civilization drowning in paganism and immorality, Paul's understanding of accountability to the one true and living God was incredibly startling. New Christians fresh from that environment could imitate Paul and show the world how faith in Christ transforms one's standing and behavior before God.

Consequently, Paul forthrightly tells us it does matter how we live as Christians. He frees us from worrying what others think about us and calls us to accept our accountability to God as a truly liberating experience.

A Trustworthy Steward

1 Corinthians 4:1–7

During a memorable summer of hard work and golf I learned something about being a trustworthy steward. Although I was only a high school kid at the time (during World War II), an older couple who owned a local golf course gave me responsibility for keeping the grass trimmed and the weeds cut. On nights when they rented the club house for social functions, I was on duty. Because I owed so much to these folks, I would never have dreamed of taking any shortcuts. Our relationship shaped my character.

Likewise with Paul. I served the owners of the golf course who had entrusted me with certain duties. Paul, however, served the Lord Jesus Christ who had entrusted him with God's secrets. Yet our responsibility was the same: to be faithful and trustworthy in the performance of our assignments.

Paul's stewardship arose from his unique relationship with Jesus. He was not a hired hand, he was a servant, or bond slave of Jesus Christ. His first response to Jesus had been, "What shall I do, Lord?" And Jesus had told him, "Go; I will send you far away to the Gentiles" (Acts 22:10, 21). Everything that followed in his life flowed from the Master-slave bond between them.

In Roman times certain slaves were privileged to oversee their master's affairs and household, much like Joseph the Hebrew slave managed the government of Egypt. But Paul was the first slave to be handed God's secrets.

What were these secrets? God was in Christ reconciling the world to himself. Paul called these secrets, or mysteries, Christ's "unsearchable riches" (Eph 3:8). God had kept these things to himself from eternity past, but now with the coming of Jesus the secrets were revealed, the mystery solved, as it were.

God had deposited the truth with Paul and the apostles. His deposit was a trust that far exceeded any human transfer of wealth, truth, or information. God's secret was wrapped up in a person, the Lord Jesus Christ. To Paul and the others God had entrusted the truth about Jesus.

At last, God's eternal plan of redemption had emerged from the old-time prophecies. With the coming of Jesus ignorance of God's salvation scheme was no longer part of the human condition.

Accountable Passion

No wonder Paul was overwhelmed by his incomparable responsibility. So heavy was this burden of trust on him that he considered himself a debtor to the unbelieving world (Rom 1:14). When it came to clarifying his role in the founding of the church at Corinth, he stripped it down to its simple essence: "I was simply doing my duty in serving Christ. I was faithful and trustworthy to him."

Paul did not own the gospel. It was given to him to give away. Looking at his story, we can easily grasp his singleness of purpose and his unswerving commitment to making Jesus known in the pagan and Jewish worlds. He challenged the synagogues and the forums. He hiked formidable mountains and sailed boisterous seas to give Jesus to people.

Paul's sense of stewardship drove him to overcome beatings, imprisonments, poor health, and vicious opposition. Nothing deterred him from carrying out his orders. Jesus had called him and had committed to him the truth about God and humanity.

Paul's truth centered on the person of Christ. Whatever he encountered, physically and spiritually, he battled with truth. As a trustworthy bond slave, he owed everything to his master and he would not disappoint him. Every Christian has received an enormously rich deposit of truth from God. What do we do with it? Are we totally trustworthy in the administration of Christ's riches like Paul was?

Only One Father

1 Corinthians 4:14–21

Paul used many figures of speech to describe his relationship to those who had responded to his gospel invitation. To the Corinthians he was both a farmer and a master builder, as well as their unique father in the faith. To the Thessalonians he was a nursing mother. Above all, he was their servant.

Despite the fact that he confronted divisiveness and immorality in the church at Corinth, these people were still his dear children. As their father in the faith, he carried huge responsibilities for their spiritual growth and development. True, resorting to hyperbole, they had had ten thousand tutors, and perhaps this multitude had impregnated the church with confusion.

Paul made it very clear that he alone was their spiritual father because he had brought them the gospel of Christ. Such a reflection would drive them back to their roots, as well as back to their pasts when they lived in spiritual darkness.

Paul cleverly used the father-child analogy to prove not only what he had done, but also what the Christians really owed him. They were low, contemptible, mere nothings before he had arrived on the scene. In sharp contrast, Paul had fathered a family of believers who were now set free in Christ and enjoying his wisdom and righteousness.

As their father, Paul had not only brought them to life in Christ, he had fed them milk. They were not ready for solid food, he judged, because of their jealousy and strife. Despite their failures, in Christ they constituted God's temple and the Holy Spirit lived in them.

Most importantly, Paul had done what all good fathers are supposed to do: he set the example and standard for them to follow. He had spent a good long time at Corinth, eighteen months at least (Acts 18:11), and then he had become an absentee father, giving correction, instruction, and encouragement by his letters. He had also sent Timothy to remind them of Paul's lifestyle and his teaching.

Life today is filled with absentee and derelict fathers, who care not for their children's spiritual, moral, physical, and emotional welfare. Paul was not like that. He never had physical children of his own, but he regarded his converts as just as precious as children of the flesh.

Paul cared for them because he was emotionally attached and spiritually concerned. He knew he was accountable to God not just for preaching the gospel but also for the spiritual nurture and growth of those who had been born again by faith in Christ.

When our children leave home there's a certain amount of heartbreak and worry. Parents do all they can for twenty or so years and then it is up to their offspring to make wise choices. Obviously, Paul's Corinthian babies would soon be on their own and he would never see them again. He no doubt suffered the same kind of emotional pulls as parents when he admonished the Corinthians to get over their fights and immorality.

What tremendous satisfaction it gave Paul to say, "You are my offspring." By linking himself intimately with the Lord Jesus Christ, he had found Christ's promise to be true: "If a man remains in me and I in him, he will bear much fruit" (John 15:5). What pleasure it gives me to recall some whom I can claim as my spiritual offspring, because God has been faithful to his promises and his Spirit has operated through his word to bring them to their second birth.

Passion for Open Doors

1 Corinthians 16:1–9

In its incomparable simplicity and clarity, the Bible uses "door" as a figure of speech for spiritual realities. Supremely, Jesus said he was the door to our salvation (John 10:7–9). When Paul returned to Antioch from his first evangelistic invasion of Asia Minor, he reported that God had "opened the door of faith to the Gentiles" (Acts 14:27).

In his Corinthian correspondence, Paul used door as a metaphor for gospel preaching opportunities (1 Cor 16:9; 2 Cor 2:12). He constantly probed the frontiers of unbelief, looking for openings, or doors, through which he could enter and bring people the great news about Jesus.

By using this figure of speech he communicated his passion to the church at Corinth and to us. It appropriately conveys the heart of his life calling. Open doors to Paul represented not only opportunities to preach and teach, but also the strategic fact that God himself worked to provide these openings for the gospel.

Rightly understood, Paul's passion for open doors relieves us of the obligation to knock down closed doors. "The Lord had opened a door for me," he explained. "A great door for effective work has opened to me," he said. At the same time, his passion tells us not to be lazy, or resigned to seeming impossibilities.

Jesus told us to "knock and the door will be opened to you" (Matt 7:7). If we are to discover God's open doors, we must adopt a compassionate, aggressive evangelistic life style. Paul set the table for us. Trudging through Asia Minor, he confronted one closed door after another until he arrived at Troas (Acts 16:6–10).

As is often the case, commercial interests show us the way. Time was when door-to-salesmen peddled products deemed necessary in every home. Insurance, soap, patent medicines, and magazines were sold this way. Christians also used this technique to do evangelism.

What we learn from Paul is not his particular method but his heart. How he rejoiced when God opened an entirely new vista for him. New energy surfaced in his heart and mind because of his passion to introduce people to Jesus.

What seems to be a closed door often yields to prayer and gentle persuasion with love and wisdom. I met a Christian man who firmly believed in door-to-door calling in connection with a united evangelistic effort in his town. His first twenty-five knocks yielded only firm rejections, but the next door opened to his knock and the family came to faith in Christ. Like Paul, he persistently pursued the open door.

Our passion does not rest in any specific method but in our sovereign God who desires that everyone be saved. In Jesus' story, the shepherd kept going until he found his one lost sheep. Such was Paul's spirit and passion. He kept going in spite of much opposition.

It's exciting to see what happens when a single door opens and entirely new networks of faith and worship develop right before our eyes. Confident that God is with us, we press on like Paul did with prayerful, persistent persuasion.

Paul modeled various roles as, like a faithful steward, he administered the riches of God's grace. As we imitate him, God will show us specific roles and opportunities to bring his grace, love and truth to others.

Today visitors to Belgium look with pain at World War I trenches where so many thousands suffered and died. As they look at the green, peaceful fields, it is hard to imagine how much blood was shed there. In our next chapter, we look into Paul's heart as he fought in the trenches, as it were.

CHAPTER 17

In the Trenches

Paul never flinched from telling what his life was like in the trenches of spiritual warfare. We don't know what he anticipated when he set out to follow Christ's mission for him, but being labeled scum was probably far from his thoughts. Did he fear encounters with "wild beasts"? Not likely. But when he wrote to the Corinthians he described some hardships specifically and some generally.

THE SCUM OF THE EARTH

1 Corinthians 4:8–13

A boat carrying Afghan refugees exploded off the coast of Australia in April, 2009, killing three of them and injuring more than 40 others. Outraged, Australian Prime Minister Kevin Rudd told reporters, "People smugglers are engaged in the world's most evil trade and they should all rot in jail because they represent the absolute scum of the earth."

When Paul called himself the scum of the earth, he did not have in mind ordinary slime on a pond, or garbage. He meant he was regarded as a low, vile, worthless, dirty, despicable, disagreeable, unpleasant, offensive, and contemptible person, a rat and a bum. Writing today, he probably would have said he was a scumbag.

We can easily understand why the prime minister called refugee smugglers scum, but why was Paul regarded as scum? How was it that the great apostle somehow merited being called the dregs of humanity?

Jesus had told Paul that he was going to suffer terribly for preaching the gospel. Jesus himself, the prince of peace, the Lord of glory, the monumental healer and proclaimer of truth, wound up being sacrificed as a blasphemer. He was treated with contempt and cruelty in spite of his conspicuous love and high moral and ethical teaching.

Likewise, Paul delivered the truth very powerfully and quite honestly and was rewarded with harsh treatment. Instead of being honored and blessed for bringing God's kingdom to Jews and pagans, he received the worst possible criticism. Paul revealed to the world God's amazing salvation by grace through faith in Jesus Christ. His reward?

A public death sentence. A public spectacle before humans and angels. A fool for Christ's sake. Weakness, disgrace, hunger, thirst, rags, brutality, wandering from place to place, hard physical labor, curses, persecution, slander, scum, garbage, the most abject of mankind.

By citing these conditions, Paul sought to wake up the Corinthian Christians to the high cost of all they had received from their commitment to Christ. They were richly endowed, having everything they could desire, and they had become proud, divisive, and contentious. By striving to expose their pride, Paul said, sarcastically, "You have come into your kingdom—and left us out. How I wish you had indeed won your kingdom; then you might share it with us!" (1 Cor 4:8, NEB).

Paul chose to reveal the literal high cost of his apostleship in his attempt to snap the Corinthians out of their self-sufficiency and high regard for their status. He designed his hardships and suffering as a shock treatment to bring the church back to Christian love and humility. He compared Corinthian pride and his trials. He used biting irony to expose their conceit. Acting like kings, they could easily wreck church fellowship, unity, and integrity.

Paul's character and commitment to Christ and his church took him through the worst of trials. Not for him were apostolic honor and privilege. His service for Christ and his church cost him physical, emotional, and spiritual pain and suffering.

The church owed everything to Paul, but he refused to fight for prestige. Reminded of the cost of Paul's service, the Christians should therefore examine themselves and stop fighting for control. Instead of acting like kings, they should follow Paul's model of service and humility. Paul yielded his rights and marched in the parade of the condemned to show us the power in his love, sacrifice, hard work, and humility. That's what being Christ's servant is like.

His Daily Hardships

1 Corinthians 15:31; 2 Corinthians 11:28

It's not uncommon today for churches to grant sabbatical leaves to their pastors, just as colleges and universities grant sabbaticals to faculty members. I've heard some grumblings from church members about this fairly recent practice, recent that is in terms of both church history and apostolic examples. Their complaint seems to be that they get no sabbaticals from their jobs, so why should the pastor.

Conscientious, hard-working pastors undoubtedly deserve a break now and then, and that's what vacations are for. But six-month sabbaticals do seem questionable, especially when we look at Paul's example.

If Paul took time off, Luke never mentioned it. None of Paul's letters contain even a hint of a vacation. Rather, in his letters to Corinth Paul singled out the weight he carried every day without let-up or relief. Not only so, he compared his daily pressures, concerns, and responsibilities to facing death.

When Paul told his followers to imitate him, did he mean to include his intense, death-like struggles for his churches? What is there about his example that we should take to heart?

Of course, pastors see here a model for their own service as shepherds of God's flock. Paul is not saying, "Now go out and work yourself to death every day." He is saying that genuine, authentic pastoring includes heavy responsibilities that often seem like facing death. He is saying that pastoring is far more than punching a time clock for an eight-hour shift at the factory or office, tough as that may be for some people.

Pastors, like other workers, can loaf if they want to. They can be casual, perfunctory, and routine about their duties. They can maintain a safe distance from the spiritual warfare that bloodies their people. They can take the easy way out when saints get in trouble, and, if they are not careful, act like the priest and Levite in Jesus's parable who avoided the mugged traveler. Paul spoke to such temptations when he compared his work to death-like demands on his body, soul, and spirit.

But how is he the model for lay people? Concerned Christians go far beyond attending services, classes, and social functions. No pastor can possibly come alongside every hurting church member. He sets the pace for others to follow. To follow Paul, every Christian must get "down and dirty" in the struggle for souls.

Paul loaded his letters with appeals for Christians to help, serve, and pray for one another. "One another" saturates his letters like a drenching downpour. Church was never intended to be a lone wolf activity.

In Paul's favorite analogy, he compares the church to the human body. Each part needs every other part. To carry one's part it is often necessary to get as overwhelmed as Paul was with daily pressures. His example transforms routine church life into something like a MASH unit. There is never a let-up in casualties from the front. That's why Paul emphasized "every day."

Of course, God gives his saints chances to take breaks away from death struggles. Jesus told his disciples to rest. Surely Paul took his rests. But the predominant motif of his life was his incessant struggle for victory in the trenches of spiritual warfare. In that we can surely follow his example.

Fighting Wild Beasts

1 Corinthians 15:29–34

According to an ancient legend, the Romans threw Paul into the arena with the lions, but when the lions approached him they retreated and refused to attack. This story adds a dramatic twist to Paul's simple statement that he fought wild beasts in Ephesus. Because Luke the historian did not include this drama in the Book of Acts, scholars conclude that Paul spoke metaphorically of his struggles there.

Even though we do not have specific details, he did not exaggerate when he compared his struggles in Asia to a fight with lions. In Paul's Second Letter to the Corinthians (2 Cor 1:8–11) he said he faced such overwhelming hardships and pressures that he thought he would die. He fought in the arena against what he called "a deadly peril."

Whatever his fight was, and whoever his enemies were, Paul said he faced danger every hour of every day. Of course, he did not die every day physically, but his spiritual warfare was so intense that he compared it to death. His foes jeopardized both his body and his soul.

Paul's striking imagery drove home his basic argument in defense of the resurrection. Here we discover plainly what motivated him. Why would he endure such savage treatment if the dead are not raised? A person would be foolish to lay his life on the line for Jesus every day if there is no hope beyond the grave. Better to eat, drink, and be merry, because death ends everything.

Paul chose the alternative because he had learned the Jesus way. Jesus made it abundantly clear that following him would bring persecution and suffering. Discipleship means cross-bearing every day, he said. Paul heartily endorsed this theme. Commitment to Christ means commitment to suffering.

To those who denied the resurrection of the body, Paul applied the logic of his own experience. He said, in effect, that he or anyone else would be a fool to suffer and die for Jesus if there were no resurrection.

Suffering has a way of purifying our motives. Paul did not suffer to be a hero, but to be faithful to Christ's calling. When the going got rough, he was driven to ask himself, "Why am I taking this abuse every day? Because I know I will be raised. The resurrection makes it worthwhile."

No Roman citizen would be compelled to fight in the arena. Yet Paul was compelled by an even stronger "law," as it were, the law of his love for Christ. Some of the "lions" who did attack him sprang from both religious and commercial interests. Paul's gospel threatened their strongholds and in city after city they plotted against him.

The applied gospel exposed both civil and religious corruption. Paul and his companions were recognized as troublemakers because they upset the status quo and challenged cherished beliefs and rituals. No wonder he felt as though he were a gladiator in the arena.

Paul's brutal honesty risked deterring some would-be followers of Christ. But he never backed off from telling the truth about the perils of genuine discipleship. I was once accused of being in a certain ministry because of what I could get out of it. The charge forced me to think about my motives, because I certainly was not in it for the money.

Peter compared Satan to a "roaring lion" (1 Pet 5:8). Paul would say Amen to that. But however the devil attacks, Christians know that Jesus has defeated him. Paul successfully defended himself against his attackers and so can we, because the Spirit of Jesus lives in us.

Paul bared his soul not to gain pity, but to make it clear that the kind of cross-bearing discipleship that Jesus talked about will invariably bring both physical and verbal abuse. Accepting this fact is perhaps the most difficult part of following Paul's footsteps.

Grace, hope, and love burned in Paul's heart and soul. Our imitation of him moves on to these anchors of our souls.

CHAPTER 18

Grace, Hope, and Love

Grace, hope, and love set apart the Christian gospel from all other religious "gospels." Paul shows us how these critical elements of his faith provided an unshakeable foundation for his life.

God's Powerful Grace

1 Corinthians 15:9–11

"Amazing Grace" has become such a popular hit that thousands of people sing it without a clue about what grace means. The tune carries the mood of the moment, even if the theology is foreign. Singing that God's grace "saved a wretch like me" does not necessarily amount to a confession of sin and a cry to Jesus for forgiveness and salvation.

Nevertheless, grace means power because it is God's grace. It was only by God's powerful grace that John Newton was converted from a slave trader to a preacher of the gospel. Only God's grace was powerful enough to bring a killer like Paul to his knees. Only his grace is strong enough to cast away our sins and remove them as far as the east is from the west, to be remembered no more.

Paul attributed his conversion to God's grace. He never forgot the moment when he heard Christ's voice questioning why he was persecuting him. Blinded by Christ's light, he nevertheless had sense enough to engage Jesus in conversation and then to obey his orders. Christian conversion is like that. Jesus confronts us and demands an up or down answer. We can choose to surrender to him or to continue the fight. Grace makes it possible to say yes to Jesus.

Grace, Hope, and Love

God's powerful grace takes no account of who we are or what we have done. It smashes our pride and drives us to our knees. Paul knew he was the unlikeliest, least deserving candidate for conversion. Smart, moral, religious, and zealous as he was, he was totally unworthy of grace.

Grace is hard to take because the recipients need to confess they are spiritually bankrupt and need help. That's difficult for people who are brought up to excel and be number one, to be good and rich and well-educated. Who needs grace? Paul certainly didn't, until he met Jesus, and then suddenly all his good stuff evaporated like the morning fog.

But that was just the beginning for Paul. Jesus gave him a new job and he set to it with enthusiasm. Instead of flogging, jailing, and killing Christians, he became one of them and tried to convert everyone he talked to, Jews and Gentiles alike. His passion drove him to excel all the apostles. Why? Because of God's powerful grace.

Grace not only converted Paul, it also energized him to be an evangelist, teacher, church initiator, pastor, and author. Grace propelled him over mountains on foot, through stormy seas and shipwrecks, and through stoning and imprisonments. By himself he could never have accomplished so much. God's grace took control of his life, giving him both the vision and the stamina to do what Jesus had told him to do.

Looking at Paul's career, we are fully justified to attribute it to God's amazing grace. The sound of grace was indeed sweet to his ears. Grace not only charted the course of his life, it assured him of complete justification and righteousness before a holy God.

We are saved by grace, Paul declared, and we do God's work by grace. There's nothing like grace to be found in any other philosophy or religion. Paul so jealously guarded God's grace that he warned against even the slightest deviation from it and called curses down on those who refused to follow it unreservedly.

Grace was under attack in his time and so it is today. Whenever we sing "Amazing Grace" we confess there is no other way to be saved and no other way to live the Christian life and work for the Lord. The harder we work, like Paul, the more grace we receive to accomplish God's will. Nothing we have done or ever will do will qualify us to receive grace. Like Paul, we are undeserving sinners saved by God's powerful grace.

Life to Come

1 Corinthians 15:50–58

As a pastor, one of the ministries I cherished most was speaking at memorial services. Lest I sound morbid, let me explain why: People's minds were focused on one thing, death and resurrection. Is there life beyond the grave? On what basis do Christians hope to live forever?

Mine was the joyful privilege of helping mourners to fix their eyes on Jesus by affirming Christian hope. Because Jesus lives, those who trust in him will also live, according to his solemn promise.

Early Christians struggled with grief and death. They lived in a culture that had no answers for death. Even godly Jews were not sure about the hereafter. Pagan Romans and Greeks had nothing to offer those suffering grief and loss.

Paul explained his feelings with powerful consistency. He looked for Jesus to turn things upside down, not only in the here and now but in eternity to come. He claimed to have certain knowledge of what happens after death. He believed that one day the mortal will be clothed with immortality.

Paul carefully crafted his ideas with a pastor's heart and intent. For some Christians, things were so bad that they plunged into despair. They suffered physically and emotionally. Loved ones had died, apparently abandoned by Jesus. Where was Jesus when they needed him? Why didn't he save them from their dire circumstances? Paul's radical truth changed everything.

Paul didn't look to Jesus to launch some cosmic rescue mission to save his people from Rome's terrors. He pictured Jesus as the sovereign comforter and controller. Temporarily, the world had not yet bowed its knees and confessed Jesus as Lord. But the day is surely coming when Jesus will be universally acknowledged as Lord of lords.

Paul wrote vivid, dramatic descriptions. Death will be swallowed up in victory. Those who have died in faith will be changed and transported into Christ's presence. Those believers who are alive will meet him in the air. Heaven's trumpets will herald the savior's return. Whatever happens will be accomplished in the twinkling of an eye.

Very simply, according to Paul, Jesus will occupy center stage and this world's leaders will pay him homage. In the meantime, don't abandon your faith, because "he who began a good work in you will carry it on to completion until the day of Christ Jesus" (Phil 1:6).

In other words, since you know the outcome of all things, cling to Jesus for your peace, joy, wisdom, and courage. He is your total redemption for all time, not just for your time on earth. One day you will join the universal acclamation that Jesus is lord.

As Paul offered hope in Jesus, he urged Christians to focus on him in heaven. He promised them that when Jesus appears, they would appear with him in glory. He acknowledged that we suffer because we are part of creation's "groaning" for redemption. But Christians should not wait in fear, but with eager hope.

Paul sketched the broad picture of eternal life and immortality to encourage believers and to help them stand by each other in times of stress and loss. In spite of death, Christians rise above the here and now. They are people of hope, not despair, because their lives are forever locked inseparably with Jesus.

Those who lives are stamped with "we will all be changed" will endure as strong soldiers of Christ. Their composure will influence others who live in fear of what lies beyond the grave.

Lifestyle of Love

1 Corinthians 13

Paul did not just preach love, he lived it. He grasped the kernel of Christ's life and teaching and consolidated it in one word: love. Christ's love drove him to the cross. We look at his cross and his love burns indelibly into our hearts. His love attracted lepers and loose women, tough fishermen and unscrupulous tax collectors. His love released widows from sorrow and sick women from their incurable illnesses.

Looking at 1 Corinthians we see Jesus and we see Paul. Of course, Paul's love was tarnished by sin, but Christ's love was not. Paul knew hatred, murder and pride. But when Christ's powerful love transformed Paul, he became more than a flaming evangelist. He also became a model of love because he imitated Jesus (1 Cor 11:1). Paul summed his life in one word: Jesus.

Therefore, in this sense, the "love chapter" pictures Paul's experience. Before Paul tells us what love is like (vss. 4–7) he uses the personal pronoun to dramatize how love supersedes a host of Christian activities, things I assume he knew not simply from theory but from real life.

Of course, "if" sometimes indicates a theoretical act. But perhaps on more than one occasion Paul's preaching amounted to a lot of noise. His eloquence would have been wiped out by his lack of love. He certainly used his gift of prophecy to unfold scriptural mysteries, and he followed God's call with remarkably courageous, persistent, even stubborn faith. But if in so doing he neglected to love people, then his giftedness and faith were useless. So far as we know, Paul did not give everything he possessed to the poor, but he gave generously. Many times he declared his willingness to die for Jesus. Even such sacrifices amounted to nothing, if his love had vanished.

The next paragraph gives us a clearer picture of Paul's life. As we confront his record in Acts and in his letters, we are astonished at how many times he exemplified his definition of love. He walked his talk. Patience, humility, and courtesy stamped his life.

Paul never sought his own glory. He was angry at times, but anger never simmered in his soul and boiled over into bitterness. Although Paul suffered wrongs at the hands of others, he did not keep a "get even" notebook. Sin and evil troubled and saddened him, but knowledge of and obedience to God's truth delighted him. In Paul, love protected, trusted, hoped, and persevered.

In a surprising revelation about the man Paul—who pounded home again and again the primacy of faith, and who lifted Christians to take the long view of secure hope—we hear him declare that love is supreme. How so? Is this not an echo of what Jesus himself had said? As an imitator of Jesus, Paul had to say that love outranks everything else.

Yet love did not come easily to such a talented, driven individual. Paul knew the perils of pride, prestige, and anger. How easy it would have been for him to live above his converts and to ignore the poor. Yet he worked tirelessly, as well as preached, to prove that he loved them and so that he would have money to give to the poor.

This chapter is not a term paper on love, it's the story of a person whose life was characterized by love because he wanted more than anything else to be like Jesus. In his letters Paul sometimes appears to be a stern taskmaster as he tackles immorality and divisiveness in the churches. That's because Paul knew the values of what we call "tough love." Love for Paul was not sentimentality, or emotion. It was obedience to the truth. He knew how to speak the truth in love.

Grace, Hope, and Love

If we are to imitate Paul, we will recognize the pitfalls of pride and self-seeking, and choose instead the way of obedient, courteous, kind, patient, and sacrificial love.

Meditating on these aspects of Paul's life and character, we may lapse into despair because we can't match his standard. However, Paul would have us rejoice and live triumphantly because God's grace saves and empowers us, Christ's resurrection guarantees ours, and love radically changes our lives.

From these lofty concepts Paul took time to expound how and why his faith called him to be generous with his money.

CHAPTER 19

Stewardship of Money

Paul did so much more than preach tithing according to his Old Testament traditions. He showed how his stewardship of money surpassed the old way of looking at our wealth.

COMING TO GRIPS WITH MONEY

1 Timothy 6:6–10; 1 Corinthians 16:1–3; 2 Corinthians 9:6–11, 15

The conversation between one of America's leading pastors and a highly respected businessman who had contributed generously to many Christian causes degenerated into something like, "Can you top this?" The culmination of their frank talk stunned me. Finally, the businessman started to brag about how much money he had given. Whereupon the pastor delivered his coup de grace: "John," he said, "you haven't given anything. I've given my life."

The apostle Paul had given his life to Jesus. Consequently, all his money also belonged to Jesus. Deep down, Jesus had stripped him of greed and covetousness. Financial worries never plagued him.

We don't know if Paul had inherited money, or how much he had stockpiled from his tentmaking trade in Tarsus before his conversion. We do know that one of his primary ministry aims was to make the gospel free of charge. He strove mightily to avoid any hint of financial scandal. He wanted desperately to pay his own way.

Apparently the church at Antioch had sent him and Barnabas on their mission without providing a checking account at home. Perhaps the best they could do was a boat ticket and some food that would keep them for a week or two.

At any rate, they lived off the land for awhile and worked their way across Asia Minor. Later on, some of Paul's new churches sent him gifts. But he helped to establish his credentials and the integrity of the gospel by working as a tentmaker at Corinth and Ephesus. In his farewell to the Ephesian elders Paul reminded them that he had never sponged off them.

Paul gave wise counsel to the Corinthians, advising them to be cheerfully generous and sacrificial in their offering for suffering Christians. He told them to give systematically on the first day of the week, that is, as part of their worship of the Lord, thus transforming giving from a legalistic duty to the exercise of a spiritual gift. In terms of his own money management, we safely conclude that Paul practiced what he preached to the churches.

In the end, he promised, their gifts would help people in need and would inspire thanksgiving and praise in their hearts. He assured generous givers that God's grace would touch them and he would supply their needs. He compared it to generous sowing and reaping. He did not lay down rules for how much to give, but rather pointed to Christ's "indescribable" gift as the example to follow.

Paul felt constrained to warn his protégé Timothy about the risks of wealth. He vividly described what happens when money takes control of one's life. In this he echoed the repeated warnings of Jesus. Paul knew that church leaders could easily be led astray by their desires for money. If he could read today's newspapers, he would be amply justified in saying, "I told you so."

Paul regarded money as a necessity to be shared, not hoarded. He did not specify how much to spend on a car or a house. Since all of life, including our possessions, falls under Christ's lordship Christians can seek his will and be lavishly generous. Jesus who saved them will make all grace abound to them.

Sacrificially Generous

2 Corinthians 9:1–15

Not one to be embarrassed about asking people to give, Paul used considerable leverage with the tight-fisted Corinthians. He found himself in a bind because he had bragged to the Macedonian churches that the Corinthian believers (living in Achaia) were jumping at the chance to give. Apparently that was all sizzle and no steak.

Their promised generous gift had not been forthcoming, so Paul wrote to Corinth and said he was sending some brothers to collect it. He feared being "ashamed of having been so confident." He defined what Christian giving is all about: it is generous, not grudging. The spirit of the giver counts for just as much as the amount given.

Then Paul laid a mini-sermon on the Christians, showing what God has to say about sacrificial, generous giving. We get some hints in Paul's story that this was not theoretical theology with him. First, he grew up as a strict Pharisee, which meant that his tithes and offerings amounted to a third of his income. Second, as a Christian he exemplified hard work for the sake of giving to meet the needs of others. Put the two together and you have a man who was sacrificially generous, trusting God to take care of him, because he charged nothing for his services. He depended on the gifts of those in the churches who followed his example.

Paul clearly spelled out two kinds of givers: those who reluctantly give on the cheap, and those who give generously and cheerfully because they have thought and prayed about it. Doubtless because he had faced this question in the churches he visited, Paul anticipated a hard question from the Corinthians: How are we going to survive if we give away so much of our money?

Enter God, maker of heaven of earth, the one who feeds the sparrows and clothes the lilies. He will do whatever it takes on all occasions to enable you to prosper.

Never one to miss a chance to elucidate a profound spiritual principle out of an earthly experience, Paul promised that God's abundant grace would not only feed and clothe them, it would multiply their righteousness as well—a double bonus, you might call it.

"You will be made rich in every way," he said. Paul knew that when we are asked to give, our first reaction is, What's left for me? So he tackled that excuse. He pointed the Corinthians to God, who by his grace not only provides bread but also gives us peace, contentment, and a generous heart.

To solve selfishness and greed, Paul administered God's grace. To help stingy Christians become generous Christians, he told them to trust God. To his mind, you cannot talk about giving unless you talk about grace. Sacrificial generosity springs from hearts trusting God to take care of them.

Stewardship of Money

God's grace makes us generous. Paul taught this principle and he lived it. Grace giving provides for people in need, it liberates us from enslavement to money, and produces a harvest of righteousness in our souls. God uses our generosity to bless others, which in turn brings praise to God.

According to Paul, the best thing we can do with our money is give it away. Strong faith is the key to sacrificial generosity.

His Financial Scruples

Philemon 12–20

I like Ken Taylor's paraphrase of Romans 12:17 in his Living Bible (1971): "Do things in such a way that everyone can see that you are honest clear through." His command rings with Pauline authenticity. Paul also gave this command to the Corinthians twice and to the Philippians and Thessalonians and Timothy. He backed it with his own scrupulous efforts to avoid even a whiff of wrongdoing regarding financial matters.

Paul worked in an environment that often aroused suspicion of traveling lecturers. Much of the suspicion was well founded, because many of them used various schemes to gain money for themselves. Without any financial accountability they were free to hit their audiences and followers for as much as they could get.

Paul, however, marched to a different drummer and he was careful to distance himself from these charlatans. When he closed out his career at Ephesus, he reminded the church elders, "I have not coveted anyone's silver or gold or clothing" (Acts 20:33). He was so scrupulous about money that he refused to take charity for his room and board, emphasizing that he paid his own way by working as a tentmaker so he could preach the gospel without charge.

He was extremely careful to avoid even a hint of misusing other people's money. The opportunity to do so arose when he stimulated an offering for the Jerusalem church from the churches of Macedonia and Achaia. Naturally, it was assumed that the apostle himself would take charge of the money, but Paul would have none of that.

Instead, he advised the Corinthians that other brothers would accompany him, telling them, "We want to avoid any criticism of the way we administered this liberal gift. For we are taking pains to do what is right, not only in the eyes of the Lord but also in the eyes of men" (2 Cor 8:20–21). This was pure Paul at his most scrupulous.

Likewise, Paul painstakingly managed his personal finances. He provided an unusual insight into his practice when he wrote to his friend Philemon. Philemon had suffered a serious financial loss when his slave Onesimus had run away. Somehow, this slave found Paul in prison in Rome, became a believer in Christ, and ministered to Paul's personal needs.

So intimate was their relationship that Paul called Onesimus his son in chains. Nevertheless, Paul decided to send him back, even though he was his "very heart." Even in this highly charged emotional context Paul wanted to be upright and honest in his money matters.

"If he (Onesimus) has done you any wrong or owes you anything, charge it to me," Paul said. To prove his good intentions, Paul said he would sign his personal IOU. To be fair, Paul also reminded Philemon that he owed him his "very self." Whatever losses he had incurred would be more than offset by the salvation he had found through Paul's preaching.

Did Paul really intend to reimburse Philemon? Locked in prison, how could he even think about doing so? Perhaps he hoped to be released, or perhaps he could have sent funds through one of his associates like Luke. Regardless of the details, his intent was clear: he wanted to do what was right by his friend Philemon, whose services he had enjoyed through Onesimus.

Such scrupulousness about finances characterized Paul's attitude toward practical holiness. When he talked about Christians having renewed hearts and minds in Christ, he included how they should handle their money. How Christians earn their money honestly, and how they use it honestly, speaks volumes about their commitment to Christ. Our honesty in the face of ongoing dishonesty often opens the doors to faith to others who are watching us. That's what happened to Paul and it can happen to us.

The next chapter takes us to 2 Corinthians, easily Paul's most personal letter. To imitate him, we can prepare to take some hard knocks for the sake of the gospel.

CHAPTER 20

Integrity as an Ambassador

Our imitation of Paul now takes us to his most defensive letter, 2 Corinthians. Here we find him battling enemies without and within. His humanity powers through this letter, as we shall see as we develop certain crucial themes: his supreme role as Christ's ambassador, what it cost him to be his ambassador, and how he kept his integrity throughout attacks on his work.

Ambassador for Christ

2 Corinthians 5:16–21

"Ambassador: an official envoy; *esp.* a diplomatic agent of the highest rank accredited to a foreign government . . ." (*Merriam-Webster's Collegiate Dictionary*, eleventh edition).

A former colleague of mine, who grew up in Africa as the child of missionaries, became the US ambassador to an African nation. I prevailed upon him to write an article for a missionary journal I was editing, but I never enjoyed a conversation with him about what it meant to be an ambassador. In some ways, I feel closer to Ambassador Paul.

However, I do wonder why he chose that appellation for himself, among the many other possibilities before him. Clearly, Paul never considered himself a diplomat, called to smooth over misunderstandings and disputes among nations. Yet Paul's style was anything but diplomatic; confrontation and disputation characterized his evangelistic zeal.

The Imitation of Saint Paul

On the other hand, diplomats frequently broker peace agreements. Reconciliation and peace dominated Paul's thinking, so much so that he gave himself another office: minister of reconciliation. If the US ambassadors' role is to help maintain peace between the US and other nations, then the title matches Paul's role as well. He strived to bring peace between God and us.

God does not make war on us; we make war on God. In effect, our sin is a declaration of war, a rebellion against God. The Bible is packed with stories about rebellions against God, about our independent choices to reject God's good and perfect will for our own way.

Warfare underlies Paul's appeal for us to surrender and make peace with God. In his role as ambassador, Paul acts like a labor relations mediator bringing two sides to a mutually satisfying agreement. Of course, Jesus is our true one and only mediator who makes peace with God possible because by his death and resurrection he satisfied God's peace terms. Paul simply announces that the deal has satisfied God's part, so now it is up to us to accept his terms.

"Come to the peace table," Ambassador Paul beseeches us. "God has been reconciled by Christ's death and resurrection. Lay down your arms. Surrender and accept reconciliation and peace with God."

Paul's diplomatic mission carried heavy theological overtones, but at the same time it was personal. God had enlisted him in the service of reconciliation. This fact reveals God's loving heart and grace, that he would appoint someone to represent him in the highest calling of all: peace with sinful, disobedient humans is possible and eminently desirable.

Paul's evangelistic assignment, in this figure of speech, clarifies for us what gave him purpose and determination. He was under orders; passion for obedience empowered his mission. He did not travel under his own colors, but under orders from heaven. Diplomats must be careful, lest they speak for themselves and not for their governments.

Yet there is something remarkably liberating about Paul's calling himself an ambassador. He was not responsible for the message itself. Jesus gave that to him. What he needed was the discipline to deliver it accurately. That's what we need, too.

Suffering Insults

2 Corinthians 12:1–10

When our children were young, we guarded their television time, not just against sex and violence, but also against situation comedies that majored in personal put-downs. We wanted them to understand that humor has a rightful place in our lives, but not the kind of humor based on insults.

In real life, insults create pain and misunderstanding, not humor. Trying to gain self-esteem at the expense of another person is wrong. As much as we agree with this truth, we sometimes grab opportunities to strike back at other people with smart, insulting put-downs.

The apostle Paul knew how to take it on the chin both physically and verbally. He suffered reproaches from his critics as well as attacks on his life. He expressed his desire to share in Christ's sufferings, which he knew included the worst kind of insults from Jesus's accusers, judges, and executioners.

When he defended his record to the Corinthian Christians, Paul lumped insults in his list of things he suffered for Jesus. His story in Acts covers experiences he labeled "hardships, persecutions and difficulties." Not so prominent are occasions when he was insulted. The high priest Ananias inflicted perhaps the worst insult of all when he ordered his company to strike Paul on the mouth (Acts 23:2). That not only hurt physically, but emotionally.

Later on, some of his Corinthian critics insulted Paul, basically accusing him of hypocrisy (2 Cor 10:10). His letters carried weight, they said, but his stature lacked power and he was nothing but a windbag. That hurt.

Paul categorized these insults as part of his overall weaknesses. However, no one examining Paul's record could label him a weak person. Such a paradox often confuses us, because strength and power control our ambitions. Weak people are losers, so to speak.

But in God's logic, weakness leads to strength. Those who do not confess their weaknesses—especially their sins—will never find God's strength. Paul aptly pictured the ultimate divine paradox: God's power is perfected in our weakness.

Insults come to us generally because we can't hide from people who want to treat us badly or put us down. Tragically, often we suffer the worst insults in our own households, and sometimes in our church families as well.

Some people love to insult us because they know we are Christians. Their favorite sport is heaping ridicule on Christians. Often, fear of such ridicule locks our lips and keeps our light hidden under a bushel. Paul labored in a thicket of opposition and criticism, but his courage never wavered.

Paul found that God's grace was more than adequate for his insults. He walked hand-in-hand with Jesus. "Suffering insults, Paul?" Jesus might have asked him. "Never mind. Stay your course and I will more than take care of you."

The psalmists compared words to arrows (Ps 57:4; 64:3). More than once they cried out to God in their pain and confessed their hope in him. God must be our refuge and solace when sharp, painful words sting us.

Preaching with Integrity

2 Corinthians 4:1–6

Looking back over my career as a pastor, I recall occasions when total honesty proved elusive in the pulpit. Outright lies didn't tempt me. No, I was tempted to shade the truth, perhaps embellishing stories or changing a few details here and there. Insights originating from other sources could easily be passed on as my own. Perhaps the toughest tests arose when I tried to speak frankly about how the Bible addressed obvious needs in our lives and instead soft-pedaled the truth. Fear of possible negative reactions sometimes squelches the truth.

Paul's Corinthian critics leveled serious charges against him, so much so that he thought it might be a good idea to quit. But he rejected that notion out of hand, because he knew that a merciful God had commissioned him to declare the gospel of Christ and defend it with all his might. A soldier entrusted with a special mission does not run away from battle. Neither did Paul. God's enduring mercy drove him on.

Not only pastors but Christians generally also lose heart when the battle rages. Through the years the church's enemies have attacked her and tried to suppress God's truth in Christ. In this case, however, critics within the church apparently had spread stories that hurt Paul.

Their charges included "secret and shameful ways," "deception," and distorting God's word. In the heat of religious conflicts, opponents often resort to the most outrageous, unfounded charges. We call it propaganda, intended to fill people's heads with lies and whip them up against the opposition.

Paul's opponents at Corinth seemed to resent his apostolic authority. They lumped him with notorious false teachers whose teachings were intended to bring fame and money at the expense of the truth. "You're just like the rest of these deceivers," they seemed to say.

Paul did not flee the conflict. He did not smooth talk his way to make friends in Corinth. Rather, he said, he totally rejected the shameful methods of other itinerant teachers. He did not distort God's word, but declared the truth openly and plainly.

Such confidence in God's word served to vindicate Paul. He defended his record before his fellow Christians and before God. Such opacity surely disarmed his opponents, who would be convicted of cooking up false charges against him.

Paul summarized his case with a stunning rejection of selfish, underhanded tactics. No love for personal wealth or fame motivated him. A fellow Christian worker once accused me of being in a fundraising effort for what I could get out of it. At times the larger vision escapes us. Paul showed us how critical it is to keep Jesus firmly in the center of our ministries, whatever they may be.

Paul followed two principles: he did not exalt himself, he exalted Jesus; he did not serve his own ends, he served other people. Congregations, individuals and agencies must work hard not to promote their own agendas, but instead promote Jesus Christ as Lord and savior, with servants' hearts. Paul spoke from the evangelist's perspective, but his attitude covers all aspects of Christian service. Honesty, truth, genuineness, and integrity should blanket all we do in Jesus's name.

Knowing the compelling love of God's calling in Christ, Paul pressed on, using spiritual weapons of warfare and finding strength in weakness.

CHAPTER 21

Motives, Strength, and Weapons

Emotionally charged because of questions about his authenticity and authority, Paul responded with answers that give us an inside the heart picture to follow in our own walks with Jesus. We learn what motivated him and how he dealt with his weaknesses and spiritual warfare.

EVANGELISTIC MOTIVATION

2 Corinthians 5:11–15

Paul evangelized because he was a spiritual debtor to those without faith in Christ (Rom 1:14–15). He evangelized because he knew firsthand both the fear of God and the love of Jesus.

His fear of God taught him that his sin had cut him off from God and nothing he could do would ever heal that wound and bridge that gulf. Sin creates a barrier that no one can surmount. Paul learned that even his rigid adherence to Jewish laws did nothing to assuage God's wrath.

Paul's knew God's holiness and justice, and his righteous judgment. He counted on standing before his judge (2 Cor 5:10). This knowledge compelled him to obey what God had told him to do—preach the gospel. To do otherwise would be utter foolishness.

For Paul, God's character constituted the starting point of his faith and ministry. Therefore, he did not rationalize or make excuses. He surmounted whatever stood between him and obedience. Considering the obstacles, that was not easy. Whenever he was tempted to choose another vocation, the fear of God rose up to haunt him and drove him to keep going.

Christ's love, as well as God's judgment, motivated and sustained Paul's evangelistic work. Never would he forget how much Jesus loved him. His love brought Paul to his knees in repentance. Christ's love converted Paul from a maniacal persecutor to a steadfast, imperturbable winner of lost souls. Christ's love shredded his pride and self-righteousness.

Christ's love caused Paul to cease living for himself and to live for him. His love emboldened Paul to preach the cross in the face of ridicule, rejection, and persecution. His love gave Paul love for others and wisdom to explain the gospel to them.

Therefore, in the end, Christ's love left Paul with no choice but to hit the road and evangelize everywhere anyone would listen, but especially in the great urban and cultural centers of the Roman Empire. Jesus liberated Paul with his all-encompassing love.

Paul held his fear of God and the love of Christ in perfect balance. To some observers, he appeared to be unbalanced, or out of his mind. People might well ask Paul how he managed to hold so keenly to apparently contradictory concepts.

Properly understood, Paul's fear of God found release and comfort in Christ's love. Paul knew God not simply as his judge but also as his lover. He found more than sufficient reasons to appeal to people to be reconciled to God. He could teach both Christ's love and God's judgment of sin on the cross.

In Paul's mind, Jesus died to save us from ourselves and from God's righteous judgment. Among his listeners were those who repented because of imminent judgment, while others turned to Jesus because they heard of his love.

The gospel message, if it is properly presented, includes both truths. To be motivated to declare that message, we are called, as Paul was, to be faithful to the fear of the Lord and to the love of Christ.

STRENGTH IN WEAKNESS

2 Corinthians 12:1–10

Probably nothing was more counter-cultural in Paul's life than the way he looked at his weaknesses. When we consider that he actually wanted to brag about them, that he saw them as an opportunity to display Christ's power, and that he actually delighted in them, we are staggered.

Paul turned our view of weaknesses upside down, inside out. Just as Jesus radicalized people by exalting humility, servanthood, and poverty of spirit, so Paul radicalized his contemporaries by refusing to knuckle under to his weaknesses.

Among his weaknesses he listed his thorn in the flesh—an illness of some kind—of which the Lord chose not to relieve him in spite of his pleadings. To his chronic pain Paul added such generic weaknesses as insults, hardships, persecutions, and difficulties.

Our purpose is not to dwell on those things that Paul characterized as weaknesses. (See 2 Corinthians 11:23–33 for the grisly details.) Rather, the key for us is to discover how Paul handled these things in a way so differently from the way we usually do. As Christians, we sometimes fall into bitterness toward God and complain about our hardships to him and to others. Often, we do not take a positive view and may in fact become quite negative and critical. Something unexpected takes our faith and smashes it against the rocks of reality like the monster billows of a nor'easter smack ships against Maine's rockbound coast.

Paul enunciated the ultimate paradox when he said, "For when I am weak, then I am strong." How so, Paul? What was your secret?

Number one, he did not count his physical condition and the comforts of life as the prime issue in his thinking. The material took second place to the spiritual. Jesus told his disciples not to be troubled by their dire circumstances, but to believe him and his promise of eternal life. Their hearts were fixed on the here and now. Jesus pointed them to life's eternal dimension.

Just so with Paul. He looked beyond his illness, his floggings, stonings, and shipwrecks to Jesus and the absolute certainty of eternal life with him. Jesus taught that life's meaning is not found in what we possess materially. Paul anchored his faith in the one who had spoken to him, believed in him, and comforted and guided him.

That's why Paul prayed the way he did. Persistent prayer led him out of the doldrums of persecution and pain into the glorious power of Jesus. Because he prayed, Paul received a word from the Lord that gave meaning to his pain and suffering.

God's outlook on life separates the divine from the human. On the human level, no one actually believes that the way to power is through weakness. No, the way to power is through superior strength and cunning. God chooses otherwise. To the weak and the suffering who seek his face he speaks reassuring words of comfort and love. "Don't worry," he says, "because you will see my power shown in your suffering."

Motives, Strength, and Weapons

Paul saw through his weaknesses and found Christ's power. If accessing Christ's love, wisdom, and power becomes our main objective and concern, then whatever we are called to endure for him is well worth it. We can know the exquisite delight, as Paul did, in finding strength, hope, courage, and faith in our weakness.

His Weapons of Warfare

2 Corinthians 10:1–6

Having the right equipment makes all the difference in the world, whether you are a carpenter or a painter. I was neither of those, but when I was a kid the golf bug bit me and infected me. I was helpless to resist, but I was ill-equipped to play. I banged around our backyard with a rusty old putter.

Driven to succeed, I saved money by selling golf balls I found in the creek and hayfield that bordered a local course. My eyes were fixed on a two-iron in the Sears catalog. Eventually it arrived and my optimism surged as I headed for the nine-hole course and played the whole round with one club, my two-iron.

Likewise, Paul's passion to succeed in his spiritual battles drove him to use the right equipment. However, unlike me, he had choices in equipment, because human weapons prevailed in his kind of warfare. Throughout the Greek and Roman worlds intellectual and spiritual gladiators vied for audiences and followers. They debated for hours on end, making points and earning cheers and boos.

Paul had their kind of equipment at his disposal, because he was a learned Jewish intellectual who excelled in debate and drive. He had studied with the best and he knew God-centered theology backwards and forwards. He exceeded the pagan philosophers in his zeal, because when the Christian church rose up to challenge his assumptions he persecuted his critics.

After he changed sides, Paul could have used the same tactics, which he labeled carnal, or fleshly. He knew where such equipment originated, and it was not from God. It was from the sin-stained human will, from hearts that were far from God and in fact did not know God.

So when he entered the arena of thought and debate, Paul chose instead to use what appeared to be ridiculously weak equipment. His weapon was the spiritual replica of a single-shot shotgun, namely, the death and resurrection of Jesus Christ. Paul steadfastly refused to preach, debate, and instruct with any other weapon than the gospel of God's saving, forgiving grace.

Going into battle, he explained what his weapons were not: "We do not war after the flesh" (2 Cor 10:3, KJV). To reject human weapons required huge amounts of faith and courage on Paul's part. He knew his formidable opponents very well: sophisticated pagans and deeply entrenched Jews. To them, his weapons were like popguns. To them, Paul fired blanks.

But Paul was utterly convinced that his weapons would prevail. He described their power and effectiveness in cosmic terms. He fought for more than churches in Rome, Ephesus, and Corinth. Paul's weapons carried universal power.

In fact, Paul's weapons of spiritual warfare surpassed anything known to the human race. He exulted in weapons that could bring every human thought under Christ's control. Whatever human philosophy or religion tried to stand up against God was doomed to failure.

Paul knew the effectiveness of the armor he took into battle. Such confidence drove him against enemies who not only debated him but also tried to kill him. Even such terrifying strongholds wilted before the magnificence of God's power in Christ.

All Christians face various enemy strongholds. Spiritual warfare is serious business, far more serious than trying to knock a golf ball into a little hole in the ground. Later in life, I thanked God for a good set of golf clubs. I also thanked him for giving me confidence to take Jesus into battles for the hearts and souls of men and women.

Paul's obedience cost him dearly. As we shall see, he was a broken vessel with a heavy heart, yet God renewed his spirit every day.

CHAPTER 22

Costly Obedience

Jesus had made it clear to Paul that his calling and commission would bring pain. In Luke's story in Acts, he does not dwell on pain, although advancing the kingdom did bring conflict. However, in 2 Corinthians Paul chose to talk more about what his obedience to Christ cost him.

THE CLAY JAR

2 Corinthians 4:7–12

My experience with clay pots is extremely limited. Unlike African women, my mother never carried water or produce in a crock on her head. She used crocks to store pickles and sauerkraut. However, part of my farm duties included carrying cold water in two-quart jars to the men and women sweating in the fields.

Paul said he was no better than your typical earthenware pot, which in his day was a vessel of great usefulness but had no intrinsic value like a diamond. It was just humble clay molded into a carrying instrument. Pots were serviceable but not admirable.

He chose this metaphor to prove that whatever he had accomplished had resulted from God's power, not his own. Paul followed the footsteps of Jesus, who gave God the honor and glory for his words and deeds. His authority and power came from above.

To prove that the clay jar that held God's treasure (the gospel) was insignificant, Paul confessed that on many occasions the jar was battered and beaten but somehow survived to carry the "water" of God's saving grace in Christ.

The Imitation of Saint Paul

In fact, the pot was like a vessel of death for Paul. Paradoxically, however, Paul's jar was being surrendered to death so that others might find true life. In this, once again, Paul cited Jesus as his model.

Above everything else, Paul wanted people to see Jesus in his mortal body, in his jar of clay. That's why he endured so much. He saw through his suffering and found God's purpose in all of it. Whatever it took, he longed for people to find new life in Christ.

In him we see not only remarkable faith and obedience, but a willingness to be hard-pressed, bewildered, hounded, and struck down. Paul not only refused to quit, he did not question God's handling of his case like Job of old had done. His faith took him to the place where, no matter what it cost, he was willing to be the beat up water pot, if that was what it took to glorify God.

Yet Paul rebounded with irrepressible resilience. Somehow, he emerged from each experience of suffering with a spirit that refused to surrender and quit. He said he was never hemmed in, never at his wit's end. He never felt that God had abandoned him, or had simply left him to die along the road somewhere.

I read about a young English girl in Africa who stumbled on ancient burial relics in a cave. Much to the fear and anguish of her guide, she picked up a jar to take home. He protested so vehemently that she finally threw it back in disgust. It shattered and her guide fled in terror because the girl had offended the spirits of the dead.

In Paul's clay jar metaphor the jar itself carried no magical powers. Rather, it symbolized the power to find new life in Christ when the jar releases the gospel, so to speak. Paul's jar spilled its contents and churches sprouted around the Mediterranean world and ultimately to the four corners of the globe. It reached our shores one day and touched my family and me.

Every Christian is a jar in Paul's mind. To imitate him our aspiration must be like his: the life of Jesus must be revealed in our jars, our mortal bodies.

His Daily Renewal

2 Corinthians 4:13–18

I began college as a Christian on a rather liberal campus where profs ridiculed what they called my Sunday school faith and tried to shake me out of it. Their intellectual offensive thrust me into my survival mode. Determined not to sink, I joined Campus Christian Fellowship.

This group belonged to InterVarsity Christian Fellowship, a national student movement dedicated to evangelism, discipleship, and missions. Meeting daily with God in Bible study and prayer constituted the key to my spiritual growth. InterVarsity called this discipline the "daily quiet time" and the staff gave me a book showing me how to do it. That started me on a lifetime habit.

Although my life's details did not match Paul's experiences, I resonated with him when he talked about his daily inner renewal. My life was like a summer breeze compared to the storms and trials he encountered. The bottom line for me and for Paul was that we both needed daily spiritual resuscitation to survive. He could not presume to go into battle for the Lord apart from a daily infusion of God's power, grace, wisdom, and love—and neither could I.

Paul pictured the daily renewal of his inner man in sharp contrast to the wasting away of his physical being. Considering his physical condition and his multiple sufferings, he could have surrendered his gospel ministry and returned to fulltime tentmaking. Physical troubles weigh down our spirits. They are like cinder blocks wrapped around our souls.

But by virtue of his daily draught of Jesus's eternal spring water of life, Paul transformed the weights of his decaying humanity into a vision of glory. He took his eyes off himself and his troubles and focused on Jesus. Being refreshed by his daily quiet time, he exchanged the seen material world for the unseen heavenly world. He traded the temporal for the eternal.

Paul's transforming perspective blossomed and fruited out of his daily meditations and talks with Jesus. Out of that milieu grew his conviction that his heavy troubles were like a quickly passing summer squall, just a temporary blip on God's cosmic radar screen.

His meetings with Jesus nourished his inner being and glued him to his track of obedience. His letters provide a few intimate glimpses of his prayers. Did he read through his Old Testament one chapter per day? More than that. I think he devoured the Scriptures because he often referenced the prophets in his letters.

Paul valued physical exercise, but he emphasized that a healthy spirit was far more important. His spiritual vitality depended on daily refreshing and renewal. Athletes know how easy it is to get out of shape when they quit training, even for a short time. Paul knew that without his daily meeting with the Lord he would fall far short of his divine commission.

Paul did not write a devotional guidebook and didn't have one himself. But his practices surely resembled our spiritual disciplines. Even as he carried the weight of infant churches, and fought to take the gospel where Christ was not known, he made sure to block out time to meet God in thoughtful prayer, meditation, and worship. Can we afford to do anything less?

Paul's eyes were fixed on eternal realities even as he fought temporal battles. When we meet Jesus every day, feed on him and drink of him, he lifts our temporary weights and releases us from them so we can soar to new heights of spiritual ecstasy.

How to Relieve the Heavy Heart

2 Corinthians 1:8–11

Paul was no stranger to adversity and he was not shy about discussing his near death experiences. As a pastor, I met members who were quite reticent about allowing anyone to know about their illnesses or problems, let alone pray for them. "This is just for you, pastor," they would say. "Please don't tell anyone." Somehow they missed the value and importance of what Paul practiced.

Paul strived to break down such pride and selfishness by saying that in Christ's body we stand for each other. The strength and comfort we receive when we are down inspire us to nurture and encourage someone else when troubles hit them. His reasoning was simple: God comforts us in all our troubles so that we in turn may be able to comfort one another. We fail to apply God's prescription for spiritual health if we lock up our troubles in ourselves.

Therefore, Paul openly laid all his cards on the table. An avalanche of troubles had overwhelmed him in Asia (the Roman province of that name, now western Turkey). He did not specify the precise nature of these life-threatening troubles. Whatever they were—probably his chronic illness as well as persistent persecution—they were far too heavy for him to bear and he despaired of his life.

Sickness and persecution contributed to his unbearable weight, which was made up of anxiety and fear. Whatever happened to him, it deeply affected his emotions. Depression struck him so deeply that emotionally he felt like a condemned prisoner carrying his written death sentence to the gallows. Paul had reached Jeremiah's woeful state when he cried to God, "Why is my pain unending and my wound grievous and incurable?" (Jer 15:18).

Paul never reached the gallows, although hypothetically he thought death had won. But the God who raises the dead had, in effect, raised Paul. God had delivered him from his mortal peril, inspiring Paul to believe that he would keep on delivering him in the future.

Regardless of how low Paul had sunk, he had never given up hope. He hung on by a thread, but it was strong enough to rescue and revive him. As we imitate Paul, we cling to Jesus even in our darkest hours. Paul called his God not only the God of all comfort, but also the God of hope who gives joy and peace to those who trust him.

Figuratively, having been raised from the dead, Paul considered the outcome of his experience of the too heavy heart. His main lesson: Don't rely on yourself; rely on God. Since God is strong enough to raise the dead (remember Jesus?), then certainly he can resurrect you from your impossible burden. "And, by the way, keep on praying for me."

Paul confessed the critical role played by every member of Christ's body. Not only are we called to comfort one another, we are called to encourage and pray for one another. Thus we partner with God, so to speak, in his glorious work of refreshing and restoring heavy hearts.

Paul's far too heavy burden is not unfamiliar to Christ's followers. My pastoral ministry tried to relieve people who had hit bottom. It was never an easy proposition, sometimes made more difficult when people refused to unburden their hearts to a fellow Christian. Paul's open admission of his despair, his hope in God, and his confidence in the prayers of others show us the path to deliverance and renewal.

Paul was not only a good teacher and preacher, he was also a good writer. To make his points stick, he used metaphors, as we see in the following chapter.

CHAPTER 23

Metaphors of Service

Good writers excel at using metaphors to convey truth. Paul was no exception and his metaphors give us a clear picture of what we can imitate in his life. They are not simplistic, but thoughtful and challenging.

THE AROMA OF CHRIST

2 Corinthians 2:12–17

Nothing in our experience helps us to recognize and appreciate Paul's dual role: he was both the smell of death and the fragrance of life. After all, a skunk always carries a powerfully offensive odor. Freshly-baked apple pie always produces a luscious, appetizing aroma. The same thing cannot both repel and attract us simultaneously. Why then did Paul characterize himself this way?

His metaphor grew out of a sobering experience. He briefly recounted a troubling, disappointing event, which shows how important human relationships were to him. Perhaps too often we forget that Paul needed people for companionship and encouragement.

Titus was one of his special friends and Paul had expected to find him at Troas and be refreshed, but he wasn't there. Deeply hurt and confused, Paul summoned strength to push ahead on his mission. He rebounded with a magnificent vision of what God had called him to be.

Instead of moping and feeling sorry for himself, Paul saw himself marching triumphantly in a Roman military victory parade. Instead of a general, Jesus led the procession. The customary tribute of local citizens

Metaphors of Service

included burning incense. Clouds of it filled the air, serving as both a celebration of victory and also as a means of covering the stench of death.

In Paul's picture, the parade released the splendid fragrance of the Lord Jesus Christ, king of kings and Lord of lords. Such a magnificent honor surely befitted him. As Paul marched in Christ's triumphal procession, he activated the knowledge of Christ, which he compared to fragrant perfume, or incense. This image released him from his despondency and caused him to reflect on the role Jesus had given to him.

As he thought about the fragrance of Jesus wafting all about him, Paul considered the dual nature of his being the aroma of Christ. He saw at once how paradoxical his role was. As he smelled of Christ, he smelled like death to some and like life to others. What made the difference?

The difference was not in Paul himself, but in how people responded to the good news he brought. Some people were turned off by his aroma of Christ. They held their noses and refused to accept Christ's offer of forgiveness and salvation. Others, however, took a deep breath and said this was the best thing they had ever smelled. They received the gospel by faith.

For the former, Paul's message brought death. For the latter, he brought life. Thus in his neat metaphor of himself Paul gave an unequivocal description of all humanity. People exposed to the aroma of Christ either perish or live. Paul echoed the words of Jesus in John 3:16, for example. There was no middle ground in Paul's theology or in Christ's. Hearing the gospel demands an either-or decision.

To some it may appear that Paul was presumptuous to cast himself in such a life-or-death role. He understood that Jesus had placed an awesome responsibility upon him. He wondered if he was up to the task, because it's frightening to think of the eternal consequences of one's witness.

He rejected the suggestion that he preached for money. As he celebrated his calling in Christ's victory parade, he pictured himself as God's messenger to the world, sent from God and speaking in his sight. Cast in such an elevated office, he could accept his responsibility with peace, joy, and confidence.

We can do the same in the name of Jesus and with the Holy Spirit's enabling, knowing that our aromas lead to far-reaching consequences.

The Letter Written on His Heart

2 Corinthians 3:1–6

Letters of introduction once served an important, valuable service in our culture. They paved the way for social invitations and business appointments. Such letters answered questions about your identity and your purpose. They conferred status and acceptance.

Some of Paul's enemies challenged his authority and credentials. They failed to recognize this traveling teacher and orator who brought foreign ideas about an unknown person, one Jesus of Nazareth, who had claimed to come from God with a radical message about his kingdom. The Romans had executed him, but Paul claimed Jesus had been raised from the dead. Not only so, but Paul had the audacity to say Jesus was the Jews' promised Messiah, the king of the Jews, the Son of God.

However, across the Mediterranean world, leading Jewish and Greek thinkers had dismissed Paul's championship of Jesus as sheer nonsense and offensive to Jewish sensitivities and customs. "Show us your letters," the critics demanded of Paul. Which meant, "By whose authority do you claim to be speaking? Prove that you have the credentials and sponsors that we should listen to you." For them, it was a matter of trust. They had to be careful about accepting just anyone who happened to be passing through town.

Writing to Corinthians whom he had visited before, Paul responded forthrightly and perhaps somewhat heatedly to their challenge. Those who comprised the church at Corinth apparently had been infiltrated by some unbelievers who tried to shake their faith. Some of the Christians were having second thoughts about Paul.

Paul refused to submit. Here we see him standing on his apostolic authority as God's messenger of truth. He needed no human recommendations or sponsors. It was beneath him to fall under the normal requirements. He did not actually say this. Instead, using a powerful metaphor, he told the Christians to look at themselves and at their relationship to him.

In effect, Paul said, "I don't need the expected letters of introduction, because you are all the letter I need. Far better than a written letter to hand you is the letter written on my heart. That's really what you are."

Taking his metaphor even further, Paul totally exposed himself to their full scrutiny by inviting them to read this letter for themselves. "Look at me and see if I meet all your requirements and expectations. I am not hiding anything. Look at me and you will see yourselves, the fruit of my labors."

Paul took a huge risk, but he used a two-edged sword in his defense. On one hand, rather than coming to Corinth, making some converts, and leaving town, Paul had embedded them in his heart. He did not use them, he loved them. They stood together in Christ. On the other hand, he invited a thorough investigation of his letter, as it were, not a letter written with ink on papyrus, but a Spirit-inspired letter from Christ written on his heart.

It is not immediately clear how we imitate Paul in such circumstances. We do not share his apostolic authority and mission. However, like him, Christians have been given certain orders from Jesus. We are to love and obey him, regardless of our circumstances. Jesus thus produces spiritual fruit in us, "letters," if you please, for all to examine. Can we be as confident as Paul was when people examine our hearts? What do they "read" in us? Genuine love, or hypocrisy?

Tough Love

2 Corinthians 7:2–16

The first rumors I heard disturbed me, especially because of the friendship my wife and I enjoyed with this couple in our church. Gossip had it that he was seeing another woman, who was known to us and his wife. Sadly, the reports proved to be true. He admitted the affair and dropped out of church. It fell to the church council to discipline him and he was dropped from membership.

Paul faced a similar situation at Corinth, although it is not clear that the offender was the man charged with incest (1 Cor 5:1). Whatever the case, discipline was required and he did not shrink from it. The tone and spirit of his reflection on this episode reveals the pain brought by tough love.

Paul knew that by demanding action in the church he risked wounding people he deeply loved. "Make room for us in your hearts" was his plaintive plea for assurance that their relationship had not been ruptured by his action toward the offender.

Paul's love for the purity of the church overruled the chance that he would lose the love of some people. He refused to allow his deep personal feelings to stand in the way of cleansing the church of Christ. Having written his letter calling for discipline, he waited for some word of response, living with the tension of uncertainty. No split-second emails allayed his fears.

He admitted his instructions hurt and caused sorrow. Yet his conscience was clear because he had not exploited anyone. Sometimes situations calling for action only serve to induce pride and power in leaders. Not so with Paul. Paul acted with love and humility. In return, God gave him joy greater than before.

God's grace works in such indefinable ways that when Paul took the hard road, and caused pain, God blessed him with peace, comfort, and joy. Tough love brings its own unique rewards.

Paul rejoiced not only because the Corinthians had not rejected his counsel, but also because they had learned something about repentance. His love affair remained intact and the Christians produced substantial spiritual fruit. The cliché "No pain, no gain" applied to the church at Corinth.

To Paul, love and discipline were not antithetical. He understood that his love for the church at Corinth required dealing with an unrighteous situation. Paul knew that God had told the Israelites, "Be holy, because I am holy" (Lev 11:44–45). In Jesus he saw God's holiness personified. Therefore, his people were expected to be holy. Violations called for repentance and restoration.

Not only was holiness in the church preserved, Paul's love affair with the Corinthians was strengthened. Healing brought mutual respect, trust and love. Had Paul not acted as he did, the situation would have festered and ultimately smeared the church's reputation and the name of Christ.

This episode stretched Paul's heart and his faith. When his preaching led to conversions and the establishment of a church, he built and nurtured bonds of love with his people. He was not just a professional revivalist; he made room for people in his heart.

My friend who was barred from church membership later repented and returned to his family and his church. His wife and children suffered grievously in the interim, but, like Paul, they rejoiced with supreme joy when he confessed his wrongdoing. Also like Paul, they never gave up on him, continuing in love, hope and prayer while God's grace worked its power in his life.

In 2 Corinthians Paul bounced from one theme to another and we struggle to find his connections. Apparently he was so overwhelmed that he simply put his pen to papyrus and poured out his heart, even if made him look like a braggart.

CHAPTER 24

Bragging and Suffering

Paul claimed he did not want to brag, but he did anyway. How and why did he do it? The answers in this chapter guide our thoughts along paradoxical paths. Following Paul's logic, we gain strength and aptitude for our own bragging, as it were.

BRAGGING RIGHTS

2 Corinthians 10:12–18

When I worked as the editor of a world missions newsletter, some agencies insisted on their bragging rights. For example, if we reported a breakthrough for the gospel somewhere in the world, occasionally we would be informed by another agency that they had been there first. Of course, I was concerned about the accuracy of our news, but I was also troubled by institutional pride.

Paul faced a similar competitive spirit in his work. Reluctantly, he was drawn into defending his bragging rights, as it were. The last thing he wanted to do was boast about his accomplishments, but he was driven to it because his authority was being questioned. The time had come to tell the Corinthians that it was indeed proper to look at his record and compare it with others. How Paul did this reflects his character and guards us against presumptive pride.

Competition for first place is unseemly in Christian work and Paul, at first, refused to be drawn into it. He showed how foolish human comparisons were, because there was no objective standard of measurement. God's standard had to be used. In that case, Paul willingly stood up for his record.

The Imitation of Saint Paul

Paul defined his mission not in terms of relative success but in terms of accomplishing what God had laid out for him to do. The only thing that mattered to him was working the field God had given him. His field included Corinth.

When Jesus told Paul what to do, Paul determined to obey. Like the chains measuring ten yards and a first down in a football game, God's will stood as his measure of success. He rightfully claimed that God's will had taken him to Corinth. He refused to take credit for the work of others.

Instinctively, it seems, something inside Paul compelled him to drive beyond the ten yards represented by Corinth. He fought on to touchdown territory that no one else had yet reached. That kind of bragging was legitimate. But he could not reach the end zone alone. He needed the growing faith of the people he loved and served.

Paul flatly rejected boasting just to thrust himself ahead of others. He elevated boasting to the ultimate standard: God's recognition. He reached back to the prophet Jeremiah, who had warned prideful Israel to boast only in God. Human recognition disappears as quickly as the setting sun. Acclaim shines momentarily and then it is gone. Only God's acclamation lasts.

In a testy situation, Paul exhibited both proper pride and proper humility. He did not back off from recording his successful work, but his goal was not to thrust himself above other workers. His competitive spirit was not fired for the sake of outdoing others, or for insisting to the Corinthians that they give him a blue ribbon, first place honor.

However, he could and did boast in the Lord because he had succeeded according to God's standard of measurement. Nothing else mattered. Even the thought of moving into new fields reminded him that he should not claim the work of others as his own.

Christian competition frequently degenerates into prideful possessiveness. Too often, it appears, we hear about "my" work or "our" work. Sometimes the demand for more workers and more money drives agencies to show they are better and more productive than other agencies. Such a spirit would be quite foreign to Paul.

Our only measurement must be against what God calls us to do, not how we stack up against others.

SUFFERING INDEX

2 Corinthians 11:21–33

Where I live we do not relish hearing our summer weather reports, because they include an index of suffering called our heat index, which combines temperature and humidity. When our index reaches unbearable, we take refuge in our air conditioning.

In a way, Paul's suffering index reached unbearable in my book. And he could not flip a switch to gain relief. I can't read his index without feeling uncomfortable myself. I feel like a piker compared to him, especially when I complain about minor discomforts.

Just as Jesus had advised his disciples to prepare for persecution and suffering, so he also forewarned Paul that he would take some hard blows for his sake. No reasons were given. It was just assumed that once you took on the name of Jesus, you would become a target of all kinds of mischief and tribulation. Paul took this to heart when he instructed his converts to expect suffering as part of their calling to follow Jesus. "You are called not just to believe, but also to suffer," he said (Phil 1:29).

Paul stands as the New Testament's example of Job. But a huge difference colored their outlooks. Job was a righteous man, but he suffered anyway. By his reckoning, that's not the way it was supposed to be. The godly didn't suffer, only the ungodly. He couldn't get God to explain why he reversed the rules in his case, so in the end he capitulated in humility, praise, and worship.

For New Testament saints like Paul, the rules changed radically. Those people committed to Christ were, in effect, promised suffering as part of their faith bargain. Faith was not an escape from suffering; it was a ticket to suffering.

With this understanding, Paul did not argue with God like Job did. True, he asked God to relieve his perpetual "thorn in the flesh," but he never cried, "Why me, Lord?" He had checked in with Jesus and so was not surprised, overwhelmed, and disappointed when opposition flared up and struck him in every imaginable way.

The writer of Hebrews warned against the devastating effects of what he called the "root of bitterness" (Heb 12:15). Noticeably absent in Paul's life is even a hint of bitterness. By refusing that road, Paul exemplified the spirit of Jesus when he suffered without complaint.

What were the results of Paul's suffering index? What did it accomplish? In 2 Corinthians 11 he cited his suffering index to prove the genuineness and legitimacy of his apostolic work. False apostles, inspired by Satan, sought to undermine his authority. Paul guarded his integrity like a mama bear guards her cubs. Whatever it took, he would not allow his converts to be subverted and turned from Christ.

Paul's suffering index also proved that he himself was for real. Peter used this principle to help his readers understand their sufferings. He said they were being purified, or authenticated, like gold going through the fire. Hard medicine, to be sure, but that's how God works with people of faith.

Paul's willingness to suffer proved how much he believed in what he was teaching. He put his life on the line because the gospel was more than worth every ounce of suffering. Martyrs send the same message: they die for their faith.

In his day, Paul sought imitators. What a powerful example he set for them to follow. In our day, as we contemplate his suffering index, we say to ourselves, "If Paul could do it, so can I."

Boasting Index

2 Corinthians 12:1–10

For someone who eschewed boasting, Paul did an exceptionally fine piece of boasting to the Corinthian church. Nineteen times in 2 Corinthians 10–12 he boasted about his work, his suffering and his weakness. In previous chapters we have examined how and why he boasted about his work and his suffering. Here we take a look at how he chose to "glory in (his) infirmities" (12:9, KJV).

There is nothing more antithetical to our way of life than to brag about one's weaknesses. Our culture's attitude is epitomized by the power of being perfectly strong, not weak. We often taunt people with physical weaknesses. We excoriate those with moral weaknesses. We shun losers and flatter winners. Renowned professional baseball pitcher Satchel Paige was honored and fawned over while he whiffed opposing batters with alacrity, but when his arm went limp his followers deserted him. Satchel never said, as Paul did, "When I am weak, then I am strong."

Paul did not compile his weakness index like he did his suffering index (2 Cor 11:21–33). Rather, he cited what his boasting index did not include and what it did.

He refused to boast about the special revelation God had given him. We're not exactly sure what Paul saw in "the third heaven," but it was something so extraordinary he could very well have bragged about it. For a moment he thought about boasting about his vision, but disregarded the idea as very stupid.

From his experience we gain another insight into Paul the man and messenger. Think for a moment how he could have used his vision in his preaching. "Come to hear a man who got a glimpse of heaven," his promoters would shout. Great crowds would follow.

"No way," said Paul. "I do not want anyone to think more highly of me because of this experience. I will stand on my own record of what I have said and done." His stance rebukes those who promote themselves and their work because of special revelations or miracles.

However, Paul did boast of his weaknesses, including his chronic illness, so that he could testify—not to a taste of heaven—but to a taste of Christ's power. "Weaknesses" is probably a catchall for everything from insults to persecution. Whatever they were, they could easily have overwhelmed him and diverted him from his work.

Our physical ailments test our spirits and so Paul was tested by his thorn, perhaps poor vision, or, as some think, recurring malaria. Whatever it was, it drove him to Jesus for healing and he got his answer: "No."

Rather than quit, Paul lived with his disability and went about his work. However, he more than lived with it; he overcame the drain of disability because Jesus gave him the power to do so.

Paul thus learned another grace lesson that transcends our human understanding: how power is perfected in weakness. The unbelieving world knows nothing about this. Weakness is weakness, period. Not power. Christians, however, know with Paul that Jesus works through our weaknesses to demonstrate his power.

Paul's formula: my weakness equals Christ's power. How did he "gladly" brag about his weaknesses? Because that's how he found Christ's strength. Two of Paul's words stand out in sharp contrast to our predictable responses to our weaknesses: "gladly" and "delight." When we can say those words, we have become true imitators of Paul.

The Imitation of Saint Paul

A number of significant themes emerge from Paul's letters, themes that he expounded in almost every epistle. One theme that stands above everything else is his magnificent portrait of the Lord Jesus Christ. His portrayal of Christ anchors the Christian faith. Beyond Paul's doctrine, however, is his love affair with Jesus. In the next chapter we look into the heart of this relationship.

CHAPTER 25

Jesus Is Everything

We advance now to Paul's briefer letters, which follow a similar pattern: a blend of sublime theology, followed by what he called exhortation and edification. But they do not read like classroom notes because they are packed with the passion of his heart, soul, and mind: his Lord and savior Jesus Christ. In this chapter we shall look not just at Paul's picture of Jesus, but also at the intensity of his love affair with Jesus.

THE EXALTATION OF CHRIST

Ephesians 4:7–16; Philippians 2:5–11; Colossians 1:15–20

"For I resolved to know nothing while I was with you except Jesus Christ, and him crucified" (1 Cor 2:2). "The life I live . . . I live by faith in the Son of God, who loved me and gave himself for me" (Gal 2:20). "For me, to live is Christ . . ." (Phil 1:21).

Paul packed his letters with affirmations about Jesus. Passion for Jesus permeated his life, his thinking and his mission. He is our example par excellence of how to plumb the depths of Jesus, who is the way, the truth and the life.

It was not always so for Paul. As a zealous, self-righteous Jew he hated Jesus and persecuted those who followed him. Jesus took that personally. He asked Paul why he was persecuting him. Such was the beginning of Paul's love affair with Jesus.

From that moment on Jesus became the central figure in Paul's life. When Jesus told him what to do and how he would suffer for him, Paul agreed and charted his life's course accordingly, even though it meant offering salvation to the Gentiles and thereby facing the wrath of many of his fellow Jews.

Knowing that Jesus was the touchstone of hatred, vilification, stoning and prison never deterred Paul. He bravely flew the flag for Jesus and accepted the challenge of the storms that blew up.

Wherever he went with Jesus, Paul encountered some folks who were glad and some who were mad. To those who decided that Paul spoke the truth he expounded the virtues of Christ for personal living and corporate church life. He presented Jesus as lord of everything and the one who transforms sinners into saints.

Paul's doctrine and experience of Jesus encompassed all of life. Jesus not only forgave sins and guaranteed salvation; he also entered every conceivable corner of a person's life. Paul offered the Christ who made and sustained the world. He pictured Jesus at the head of a cosmic victory parade over all the forces of evil. Paul's Jesus brought immortality to light. Jesus spelled the end of the fear and sting of death.

In Paul's mind, Jesus radically changed relations between masters and slaves, wives and husbands, parents and children, men and women, Greeks, Romans and barbarians, and between Jews and Gentiles. In Christ's body, the church, Christians enjoyed Christ's acceptance and his gifts.

Paul the theologian created his magnificent vision of Jesus so that the facts would change people. "Let this mind be in you which was in Christ Jesus" (Phil 2:5, KJV) shows the way to humility and unselfishness, for example. Supremely for Paul, Christ's death and his becoming sin for us shows us how to deny ourselves, put ourselves to death as it were, and follow him.

Because Jesus was alive and not dead, Paul longed to be with him. Paul strived to know Christ's suffering and his subsequent resurrection power. He prayed to grasp all the dimensions of Christ's love, which he admitted was beyond human understanding. Such love also energized his witness throughout the Roman Empire.

Paul also gladly accepted Jesus as the one who would be the final judge of his work. More than anything else, he wanted to hear Jesus say to him, "Well done, good and faithful servant." He awaited his crown of righteousness.

Coming to grips with Jesus is a total experience of trust, obedience, and temporal and eternal rewards. That's how Paul shows us the way. That's

Jesus Is Everything

what he wants us to take away from his letters. He wants us to share his passion for Jesus, which puts him at the heart of everything.

Vision of Jesus

Colossians 1:15–20

Millions around the world have read Josh McDowell's book, *More Than a Carpenter*. He tells how he secluded himself in a hotel room for two days with twelve legal-sized tablets and in those forty-eight hours he wrote his book about Jesus. Never in his wildest dream did he expect that his Jesus story would attract such a wide audience, including millions of people belonging to other religions.

Paul's original vision of Jesus was rather more dramatic. He was knocked down and blinded by a brilliant light, but nevertheless he clearly heard Jesus speaking to him. He followed the Lord's orders and the rest is history, as they say.

But Paul never wrote a systematic life of Jesus. He preached Christ's death and resurrection—the power of his cross—as the only way one can gain forgiveness, God's righteousness, and eternal life. When Paul sat down to write to his churches he penned the most magnificent portraits of what Jesus meant to him.

Paul used his pictures to portray theology and practice, creed as well as conduct, belief and behavior. He did not write either biography or systematic theology. Paul's knowledge of Jesus, and his obedience to him, motivated him to develop the same intimacy with Jesus among the Christians in the churches.

Somehow, Paul combined personal passion with the loftiest philosophical concepts when he wrote about Jesus. Yet his relationship with Jesus broke the bounds of human understanding. For example, how could the creator and sustainer of the universe shed his blood on the cross?

Paul's revelation of this mystery proves that he dwelt on the most intimate terms with the one who had redeemed him. Imagine, if you can, locking yourself in a study for a couple of years and coming out with anything even close to what Paul had to say about Jesus. Where did Paul gain his insights? Prior to his missionary travels Paul was immersed in extremely intensive hours of prayer and meditation. His own explanation is that God revealed Jesus to him during his three years in Arabia, preparing him to preach to the Gentiles (Gal 1:15–18).

Paul did more than study what God had taught him, he lived it and taught it. He prayed that the Colossians would somehow grasp Christ's glory and majesty so that they might please God with their strength, growth and fruit—as he himself had done. Simply put, Paul had found that his personal key to spiritual growth and success was his vision of Jesus.

He knew that pleasing God in everything begins with looking at all of life through the Jesus lens. Paul's focus on Jesus and his knowledge of who Jesus really was kept him solidly fastened to his mission in life. When things got rocky, as they often did, he rehearsed in his mind the magnificence of Jesus.

God's fullness lived in Jesus. Jesus controlled everything in the world and the church. Jesus died on the cross for him. Jesus gave him peace with God. That was more than enough to sustain him in his dark hours. So it is with all of Christ's followers. Clinging to what they know about Jesus, they defeat circumstantial enemies that would drag them down.

Colossians 1:15-20 pictures Jesus in 111 words. What can we write and tell about Jesus, as Paul did, in one hundred words or so? Paul's vision of Jesus staggers us; it drives us to keep Christ's glory and greatness always before us.

Pressing on to Jesus

Philippians 3:7–14

From what we have already discovered about Paul, his monumental passion was to destroy Christians (Acts 9:1–2). His strict religious heritage and training drove him to fierce, intense persecution (Phil 3:4–6). From that standpoint, we can easily say that Paul had his life together. He polarized everything around a single objective.

But then Jesus accosted him and Paul discovered a life-changing North Star: Jesus himself. He hurled his old passions and accomplishments on the rubbish heap, absorbing the loss of everything because they were so much "dung" (KJV).

On the balance sheet of his life, Paul wrote off his significant assets as losses. Humanly speaking, that was an extremely unwise thing to do. But Paul knew that unless he chucked his profits into the garbage, he could never achieve something far more valuable, something that far surpassed anything he had ever known before. Now on the profit side of his ledger he wrote "Christ Jesus my lord."

Gaining Jesus and finding himself incorporate in Christ superseded everything else in Paul's life. Christ gave him his right standing before God that his previous passions could not do. Here we uncover his new driving force: "All I care for is to know Christ" (vs. 10, NEB). He longed to experience Christ's resurrection power, to share his sufferings, to conform to his death, and to achieve his resurrection from the dead.

Paul pictured in graphic detail what his new commitment required, thus showing us clearly how we can follow him. Jesus had seized him and he wanted to make sure that he would fulfill Christ's total purpose for his life. That meant pressing on 24/7 for the prize awaiting him in heaven. Much of Paul's baggage was already on the town dump, but other emotional baggage remained. He pledged to forget that stuff so it would not impede his path to glory.

We can likewise orient our lives around Paul's three-fold summary: win Christ, be found in Christ, know Christ. Looking at our priorities, this demands that we jettison all claims to self-righteousness and religious heritage (even our zeal for God, if it is misdirected). Only by doing this can we hope to match the clarity and intensity of Paul's ambition.

Compelling Focus

Galatians 2:20

Spending time with Paul brings us cheek to jowl with a man possessed. Like a powerful locomotive thundering down the track, he drives unerringly according to the compelling focus of his life: Jesus Christ living in him.

Paradoxically, however, Paul was dead. This fiery Pharisee, this indefatigable persecutor of hapless Christians, was nailed to the cross with Jesus. Jesus had struck him blind and confronted him on the Damascus Road with a crucifying question: "Why are you persecuting me?"

The crucified Christ had defied the powers of sin and death and now he was talking to Paul from heaven. His penetrating voice and question drove the spikes into Paul and he died with Jesus on the spot.

Paul the possessed criminal became Paul the possessed Christian, not just a follower of Jesus but a man totally owned by him. Paul no longer did what he loved to do; he did what Jesus told him to do. Body, soul and spirit he belonged to Jesus. He called himself Christ's bond slave.

Because Jesus loved Paul and sacrificed himself for him, he charted his course according to Jesus. Physically, spiritually and emotionally Paul's life became a journey of faith empowered by the indwelling Christ.

Paul was not a dummy like the Eveready battery rabbit. He suffered, he hurt, he hungered, he got angry, he was perplexed and betrayed and he endured because Jesus possessed him. Jesus, as it were, powered Paul to a life of sacrificial, faithful obedience. The life he lived was not his own; he belonged to Jesus.

Paul grasped the nettle of his Lord's uncomfortable commands: Deny yourself. Take up your cross. Follow me. His commands served as the North Star of Paul's life.

Paul's theme, or credo, sounds so simple, but it is eminently profound because it encompasses every bit of our lives. A host of difficulties challenged Paul's faith and commitment. From rejection by the early apostles to stoning and shipwreck, Paul confronted issues that would have forced less worthy followers of Jesus to surrender.

Only Paul's intense identification with Jesus kept him going. Jesus loved him. Jesus surrendered himself for Paul. In a uniquely Christian paradox, Paul died with Christ yet he was very much alive. But it really wasn't Paul, it was Jesus.

Jesus had promised those who loved and obeyed him that he and his Father would make their homes with them. Therefore, "Jesus lives in me," Paul exulted triumphantly. He had learned, as Jesus had, that the road to life passed through death.

As far as Paul was concerned, there was no secret entry point to how he lived. When he had encountered Jesus, he jumped to the challenge and took Jesus at his word. "I live by faith in the Son of God," he declared. For him, it was that simple. May it be so with us.

We confess that Paul's testimony stuns and rebukes us, because we fall so far short of his compelling focus. We can begin to capture Paul's testimony by thinking each day about the difference it makes to have Jesus living in us.

Our next chapter opens for us Paul's profound teaching about the Holy Spirit and what it means to live under his control.

CHAPTER 26

Living under the Spirit's Control

Our imitation of Paul takes us to his groundbreaking life in the Holy Spirit. Jesus had explained the Holy Spirit's work to his disciples in the Upper Room (John 14–16). In Acts, Luke describes Holy Spirit experiences, but it remained for Paul to teach the Holy Spirit's abiding presence and to live each day under the Holy Spirit's control.

EMPOWERED BY THE SPIRIT

Galatians 5:16–26

When I was a student leader for InterVarsity Christian Fellowship, the senior staff challenged me with the provocative question: What results do you see on campus that you can attribute solely to the Holy Spirit's work? I wrestled mightily with their word "solely." I knew what they were driving at. We all wanted to see results in terms of evangelism, discipleship, and world missions, but not because we had done something great. We wanted to see something that we could not account for in purely human terms.

That's how it was for Paul. After his dramatic conversion he was informed by Ananias that he would be filled with the Holy Spirit. The first sign of this was his preaching, but then he was sent home, where he remained until summoned by Barnabas.

Paul found the Holy Spirit's wisdom to help Barnabas teach the rapidly growing congregation at Antioch. But what about his calling from Jesus to bring his name to the nations and to the Israelites? The Holy Spirit had not forgotten. One day, out of the blue, so to speak, the Holy Spirit informed the Antioch church leaders that they were supposed to commission Barnabas and Saul for a new mission. The elders listened to the Spirit and let their teachers go, not knowing exactly for what purpose.

Here the Spirit interposed his leadership once again, defining for Paul and Barnabas what they should do and where they should go. The Spirit provided clear guidance to Cyprus and beyond. The prophecy of Ananias was unfolding.

Paul's Spirit-filled preaching brought many to faith, but it also aroused hostility and persecution. At one point the Spirit prohibited him from preaching in certain areas and instead directed the course of the gospel westward. Signs of the Spirit's work accompanied Paul everywhere, but when he announced that the Spirit was leading him back to Jerusalem and certain imprisonment, his friends protested and strongly urged him not to go. Despite this, Paul obeyed the Spirit's direction.

Clear evidence of the Spirit's empowerment of Paul surfaced in his indefatigable boldness in the face of constant harassment and the consequent spiritual fruit thereof. Clusters of new believers sprouted across the fringes of the Roman Empire. He steadfastly refused to take any credit for the results. New believers had to rest their faith in the truth of the gospel, not in the power of the preacher. He disclaimed any oratorical skills for himself.

Standing back from the numbers of converts and churches, we recognize the Spirit's empowerment in the way Paul handled opposition, persecution, suffering, and a host of problems in churches like Corinth. For him, being filled by the Spirit was far more than a clerical credential. Empowerment extended to every facet of his life: witness, godliness, prayer, integrity, honesty, truthfulness, and love.

For us, perhaps the most significant fruit of the Spirit's empowerment is the legacy left by Paul in his inspired letters. Even non-Christian scholars have credited his writings with skill, logic, and wisdom. For believers, they are the repository of the heart of Christian faith and practice.

Every follower of Christ stands to be instructed by Paul, not just in his theology but also in his Spirit-filled life. God provides spiritual empowerment for every Christian. It is not reserved for the special few. Paul commands us not to quench the Spirit but to be filled with the Spirit. He points the way for us to find joy, satisfaction, and completion in our various callings.

Walk in the Spirit

Romans 8:1–17

Riding a Ferris wheel feels relatively safe when you enter your cabin, which then begins its gradual ascent. But when you reach the apex and gaze out into thin air, you wish the wheel would hurry up and deposit you on firm ground. Paul's walk in the Holy Spirit was something like that.

From the Holy Spirit's initial occupation of Paul when he opened his life to the Lord Jesus Christ, the record shows that he often soared to heights of revelation and glory. But then he looked around, as it were, and saw danger and potential conflict all around.

Telling his story to the Roman Christians, Paul first unloaded the gospel of salvation by faith alone through God's grace. Having established his solid platform, Paul decided it was time to talk about what the Holy Spirit had done for him. (In Romans 8 he mentions the Holy Spirit nineteen times.)

Paul was not with the apostles when they heard Jesus expound on the Holy Spirit (John 14–16). His training in the Old Testament did not give him even a remote clue about what the Holy Spirit would do for him. How then was he so well instructed and prepared for the Spirit's work in his life?

We have to conclude that it was a matter of divine revelation for him. Paul's story shows that he not only absorbed the theology of the Spirit, he also engaged in Christ's mission in the power of the Spirit and he told his converts about a radically different way to live under the Spirit's control and guidance.

Paul's all-encompassing, driving motto was: "For me to live is Christ." If we had the chance to ask Paul how to do that, he would identify the Holy Spirit as the means. For Paul, Jesus and the Spirit are inseparable. Being occupied with Jesus, he was possessed by the Spirit, and vice-versa.

Likewise, there was no mystery with Paul about how a Christian gains the Holy Spirit. From the moment he was "in Christ" he possessed the Holy Spirit. The third person of the Trinity lived in him. Paul experienced the truth of what Jesus had told his disciples: The Holy Spirit would reveal the truths about him and be their counselor and guide (John 15:26; 16:13–15).

But at the summit Paul surveyed the world, the flesh, and the devil and decided he had to fight. He engaged in an ongoing struggle between his flesh and the Holy Spirit. This war so engaged him that he had to learn how to use the Spirit's indwelling power. He feared neglecting the Spirit and sought always to be filled by the Spirit's grace, strength, and wisdom.

The church, he realized, could never make it on its own. The powers arrayed against the church were beyond human ability to surmount. Paul learned that regardless of how hard he worked and how much he preached, he was an empty vessel apart from the Holy Spirit's direction, control, and blessing.

His bedrock confidence blossomed because in whatever circumstance he found himself, he could always cry, "Abba, Father," by the Spirit's unction. He knew he was God's child and, in the end, that was all that mattered.

Paul's story takes us to the top and back in total safety because we are in Christ. It's the Spirit's job to remind us of that in the heat of our battles.

His Fruitful Life

Galatians 5:16–26

One of the earliest lessons I learned as a new Christian was the simple, obvious truth that fruit cannot be manufactured. Having grown up on a farm, and having worked in a neighboring farmer's vineyard, that fact was as plain as the law of gravity. It is physically impossible to make a grape.

My Bible teachers took this fact and applied it to Paul's description of his fruitful life. Whatever else Paul meant, he certainly tried to make clear that the fruit he saw in his life was not something he accomplished by his own self efforts. The Holy Spirit was the producer.

But what was Paul's role in spiritual fruit production? Did love, joy, peace, patience, kindness, goodness, faithfulness, gentleness, and self-control just pop up on his plate one morning? Hardly. Were these qualities evident in his life from the moment of his conversion? Paul gives no evidence that they were.

What he does reiterate in his letters is the fundamental fact that when he submitted to Christ he became the repository of the Holy Spirit. Receiving Christ he had also received the Holy Spirit. He says that his body became the Holy Spirit's temple.

Therefore, he received the inner spiritual resources to obey the Holy Spirit, live by the Spirit, be filled with the Spirit, to walk by the Spirit, and to become a person whose life was marked by the fruit of the Spirit.

Paul's fruitful life looks more like a fruit basket than a shelf lined with nine pieces of fruit. Ranging over his experiences described by Luke in Acts, and adding his own notes from his letters, we clearly see that Paul's life was a package, or a container, into which the Holy Spirit continually poured his fruit. I do not see Paul sitting down at day's end and toting up which of the nine fruits he saw in his life that day.

Reluctant as I am to say this, it almost looks like Paul's fruit appeared automatically. However, nothing is automatic in the Christian life. We do not walk around like empty boxes waiting for the Holy Spirit to deposit something in them.

In Galatians 5:16–26 Paul emphasizes living by the Spirit, being led by the Spirit and walking by the Spirit. He lived each day totally aware of the Spirit's presence and the natural consequence was spiritual fruit, probably not limited to the nine he cited here. From his conversion on, Paul had to learn what the Holy Spirit wanted to do in and through him. Probably one of the first things the Spirit did was slow him down and restrain his impetuous spirit.

Paul was a doer as well as a thinker. We would call him an activist today. He rushed from one city to the next with the gospel, but occasionally the Spirit delayed him and then led him into many rough encounters that tested his mettle. In the crucible of suffering, as well as preaching, the Spirit produced in Paul the godly character he later called fruit.

Paul learned Christ's vital truth that fruitfulness comes from abiding in him, not from tearing up the countryside and trying to manufacture fruit. Jesus promised that those who live in him will produce much fruit. Without him, he said, life will be barren.

Paul did not drive a wedge between Jesus and the Holy Spirit. Being Spirit-led and Spirit-fruitful for him meant being fully occupied with Christ. With his eyes clearly focused on Jesus, the fruit just appeared. In this way Paul set the model for us to follow Christ and become fruitful Christians.

Paul's life was stamped by three clear convictions: he would be filled by the Holy Spirit, he would walk in and by the Spirit, and he would not quench the Spirit. His markers are the key to imitating him.

What makes the Spirit's work vividly dramatic is the change he brought in Paul's life. Next we'll see Paul in "before" and "after" photos, as it were.

CHAPTER 27

The "Worst of Sinners"

Paul would never recommend that we imitate his life before he became Christ's servant. Why then did he tell his story so often? So that, no matter what our past may include, Jesus can do for us what he did for Paul.

COMPLETE TRANSFORMATION

1 Timothy 1:12–17

Why would a holy, wise, and just God entrust his gospel to the worst of sinners? Why would Jesus judge a violent blasphemer and persecutor worthy of his trust and appoint him to his service? If we had a precious treasure to guard, we would not turn it over to a known jewel thief. We would not ask a child molester to babysit for us.

What seems foolishness to us turns out to be God's superlative wisdom. Jesus displayed Paul, the worst of sinners, to the world so that the rest of us might find hope. Imagine the store manager of Macy's taking a helpless dope addict from the streets of Chicago, decking him out in the finest clothes, and putting him on display in the State Street window.

However, Paul received something far more valuable than window dressing. God gave him the new clothes of Christ's righteousness. Jesus lavished his grace on him. Faith and love replaced blasphemy and murder. His transformation was complete.

When Paul first displayed his new clothes frightened observers shouted, "Faker." They could not believe that the worst of sinners had become part of God's plan to demonstrate his love and forgiveness. Dramatic change left them dumbfounded and bewildered.

Naturally, we are inclined to shun, stone, or lock up the worst people. They fall beyond the scope of redemption. Yet Paul of Tarsus stands before us, typical of all those in the future who would confess their faith in Christ and find forgiveness and eternal life. He not only appears in the storefront of all humanity and declares hope and forgiveness, he also shows the way to a meaningful vocation. Christ appointed his persecutor to his service.

Paul says, in effect, "Look at me and you'll see Christ's unlimited patience." Paul spotlighted God's patience because he knew he deserved his judgment long before he met Jesus. How many prisoners had he taken? How many people had died at his hands? He had tested Christ's patience and lived to tell about it.

Jesus knew what he was doing when he chose Paul in spite of his horrendous record. Jesus came to save all sinners. Paul offered his testimony to prove it. If Jesus can save the likes of Paul, he can save anyone.

Of course, some candidates for salvation refuse God's offer though their records are not as dark as Paul's. Perhaps they have achieved a high degree of morality and feel no need of God's forgiveness. Their pride and self-righteousness condemn them.

Every believer in Christ speaks to the world like the fashion figures in department store display windows. All of us manifest the boundless measure of God's love and mercy. We need not be the worst of sinners to invite people to see what Jesus can do with anyone who repents and believes.

When we appreciate Christ's patience with us, we utter a doxology like Paul did (1 Tim 1:17). The magnificent scope of his praise sets the pattern for us. The God who did the seemingly foolish thing in Paul's case must receive honor, glory, and praise because of what he has done for us in Christ.

The New Man

Ephesians 4:17–32

Jesus Christ came into my life when I was a teenager. Consequently, some bad stuff got cleaned up. I felt like I used to when I was a kid on my grandfather's farm, emerging from the galvanized tub in the smokehouse after my weekly Saturday night scrubbing. The old dirt disappeared and a new person showed up for inspection.

Paul's life-changing experience with Jesus was something like that. He did not say in Jesus's terminology that he had been born again, although that's exactly what had happened. Jesus had done something so special for him that he called it a new creation. He categorized his life as first the old Paul and then the new Paul.

Apart from his crimes against the church, Paul did not specify what sins he had struggled with. He admitted that the good he wanted to do, he failed to do, but the evil he wanted to avoid he kept on doing. He compared his struggle to warfare.

But in Christ the new Paul arrived to help turn the world upside down and to show the way to a powerfully different way to live. Instead of persecuting Jesus, he became his loyal follower and servant. Instead of dragging Christians off to prison and death, he became one of them and then told others that they, too, must become Christians.

With Jesus came the Holy Spirit to engage Paul's mind and heart. The Spirit instructed Paul in the truths and ways of Christ. The Spirit told him where to go and what to say. The Spirit used Paul to bring the light of God's truth and holiness to bear on a morally corrupt society. Such was the new person Paul came to be.

Paul's story became the pattern of his teaching. He hammered at the Christians to live like the new people they were in Christ. Paul left nothing to their imaginations. He instructed them to steer clear of lying, gossip, dirty stories, fornication, greed, indecency, lust, angry shouting and cursing, and stealing.

Paul recognized the critical importance of displaying what it meant to be made new in Christ. He urged conduct befitting one's profession of faith: tell the truth, get over your anger before sundown, work hard and honestly, share with the needy, speak blessings to one another, be tender-hearted and forgiving, live in love, be kind, compassionate, humble, gentle, and patient. Live at peace with Christ's peace in your hearts.

Such a dramatic contrast between the old and new gives us a clue to how Paul saw his personal walk with God. He would never tell someone to do something he was not doing himself. He walked his talk.

For him this called for unreserved obedience to Christ. Faced with huge obstacles, he never retreated from what Jesus had called him to do. Paul was constantly on his knees in prayer. His prayers show us what kind of a new person he was. He did not cling to his own prerogatives, but gladly yielded his life to God. He found strength in friends he worked and worshiped with. He did not go it alone.

Paul's new life is the pattern for ours. All the resources he found in Christ are available for us to enjoy as we live out the new people we are in him.

His Resume in a Nutshell

2 Timothy 3:10–17

As I write this chapter, the nation's unemployment rate sticks at 10 percent. This means many people are out of work and many people are writing resumes looking for jobs. Counselors offer instructions in how to write good resumes.

Paul never had to write his resume to gain employment. He appears in church history as a man of impeccable credentials, academically and morally. Later on, however, he consigned those credentials to the garbage dump for the sake of knowing and serving the Lord Jesus Christ.

When Paul followed Jesus into pagan Gentile territory he did not offer his resume to the city fathers and synagogue officials. If he had used a business card, it would have simply said: "Servant of Jesus Christ."

But when it came to recruiting workers, Paul was not bashful about citing his resume. In Timothy's case, he was about to follow in Paul's footsteps and Paul wanted to buttress the younger man to prepare him for rough battles in the years to come.

As we look at Paul's resume, what first strikes us is his singular lack of accomplishments. We know his outstanding record from Luke's stories in the book of Acts. In writing to Timothy Paul could have recited the many churches he had established from Ephesus to Corinth and so on.

He could have written something like: "I successfully prevented a prison break in Philippi." Or, "I held my own in the debates with the top Greek philosophers in Athens." You get the idea. This kind of credit is conspicuously absent from Paul's resume.

Instead, what do we find? His record of faithful teaching, godly character, and persecution. What we find there is the genuine article, not a piece of puffery. He needed no embellishments to enhance his standing before Timothy.

Paul did not have to write to impress Timothy because Timothy had seen it all for himself and he had been through some of Paul's tough experiences as well. "You know all this," Paul said, in effect, "but I am going to remind you so that you will know what to expect in days to come."

The Imitation of Saint Paul

Paul first cited his teaching, which he had received from the Lord. Paul's encounter with Jesus produced not only a career change, but also a profound intellectual change. His old theology was turned upside down. Salvation no longer depended on keeping the works of the law, but on receiving God's forgiveness and righteousness through faith in Christ. This was the heart of the matter and Timothy must stick to it.

Paul held up his way of life—his honesty, integrity, unselfishness, generosity, hard work—as Timothy's model. His supreme purpose was to obey Jesus through preaching the gospel. He wanted to glorify God in everything he did. His success depended on faith, patience, love, and endurance—outstanding qualities of the Christian life.

Lest Timothy think success would be handed to him on a platter, Paul reminded him of the hardships he had suffered, including his stoning at Lystra (Acts 14:19). If anyone aspires to greatness in God's kingdom, Paul's resume dispels the notion that success comes without a huge price.

Resumes do not normally highlight the applicant's rejections by the public. That is not the way to land a good position. Paul's faithfulness to his calling included suffering. His resume reminds us what to expect if we are faithful to Jesus. A godly pattern of life guarantees the devil's onslaughts

The "worst of sinners" became God's new creation. To follow Paul, we thank God the old is past and the new will bring us fruitfulness, peace, and godliness.

Our next look at Paul takes us to the cross of Jesus Christ, which became the priority and power of his life.

CHAPTER 28

The Supremacy of the Cross

The first time I slept in a hotel room in Mexico I felt uncomfortable because a crucifix hung over my bed. I had sung "The Old Rugged Cross" countless times in my upbringing, but in our family we did not use the crucifix to remind us of Jesus's sacrifice. Would Paul have done so? I don't know, but I do know that the cross was his burning passion. The cross reigned supreme in everything he taught and lived.

Boasting in the Cross

Galatians 6:12–16

The twenty-nine-foot tall, fifty-five-year-old Mt. Soledad Veterans Memorial Cross in a San Diego, California, public park has survived an eighteen-year legal battle against opponents who want it torn down. The episode revealed that the cross of Jesus Christ, some 2,000 years after his crucifixion, remains what the apostle Paul called a stumbling block. It is just as offensive now as it was in his day.

Strangely, however, Paul said he was so proud of this cross that he made it his priority in life. Of all the things he might legitimately be proud of, Paul said he would boast of nothing else. The crucified savior reigned supreme in his thoughts and his preaching. He gave the doctrine of the cross full weight when he proclaimed the gospel in regions where Jesus was an unknown person.

Why glory in something so shameful and despicable? Paul even admitted to his Jewish audiences the truth of their own scripture: "Cursed is everyone who is hung on a tree" (Gal 3:13; Deut 21:23).

Obviously, Paul knew the story of the cross. If he was studying in Jerusalem at the time he surely would have been aware of the public uproar over the fate of Jesus. Perhaps he may even have been part of the mob screaming for Christ's blood. As a zealous, dedicated Jew he saw Jesus as a powerful, dangerous threat to his established religion. Paul desired more than anything else to keep things as they were.

But Paul turned the Old Testament curse upside down when he realized that Christ's cross brought him exoneration from the curse upon all those who broke God's laws. We are not far off the mark in suggesting that this fact was probably the number one reason why Paul made the cross his priority. Jesus took the curse that Paul fully deserved, and that all of us deserve because we are all guilty law-breakers. Even if we are guilty of just one infraction, we are guilty of violating the entire code (Jas 2:10).

What Paul gloried in offends people because the cross stands as a stark reminder of their sins and what their crimes against God's holiness and purity cost him. Strictly speaking, the cross necessarily offended Paul at the outset, and so it must be today. If people do not sense their complicity in Christ's cross, they are not likely to flee to him for forgiveness and salvation.

Paul boasted in the cross because it removed the dark blot of sin on his soul and also because it empowered him to deal with contemporary sin. The cross not only freed him from guilt and judgment, but also from sin's present power. He said that because he was united with Christ in his death he had become a new person. Sin no longer reigned.

Paul likewise used the cross as a picture of his personal walk of faith with Jesus. He was crucified with Christ. He boasted in the cross because it opened the way for Jesus to live in him. The old Paul had been nailed to the cross. The cross gave him peace with God and the life-changing incentive to take its message to Jews and Gentiles alike.

When Christians properly seize and own the cross, they claim God's forgiveness and his enabling power to live a holy, God-pleasing life. Christ's cross satisfied God's holiness and justice and fulfills God's plan for the church to be the habitation of godly people.

Speaking of his cross, Jesus said, "The son of man must be lifted up, that everyone who believes in him may have eternal life" (John 3:14–15). That's why Paul made the cross his priority. He brought no other message than Christ crucified. He was proud of that disgusting symbol of God's curse and death because without it he was lost and he had no good news for a lost world.

Public symbols have a rightful place in a free society. However, more valuable and important as a witness to Jesus than a twenty-nine-foot concrete cross is the testimony of Christians who boast in Christ crucified and make his cross their priority. To imitate Paul, we must understand why the cross was so important to him. We then allow the cross of Christ to shape our lives and values as it did for Paul.

We thank and praise the Lord Jesus Christ for bearing our guilt and judgment on the cross. We pray, as Paul did, that everything Jesus did for us on the cross will be exemplified in our lives before others.

The Wisdom of the Cross

1 Corinthians 1:18–31

Paul grew up with the wisdom literature of the Old Testament. He was also well acquainted with the wisdom of the Greeks and Romans. But when Christ found him, he discovered the wisdom of foolishness.

This apparent paradox has tripped up people from Paul's day to ours. To put it simply, how can you be saved by what appears to be foolishness? Surely God's way must require the best of human wisdom.

At one point in his life, Paul tried to rub out the foolishness of the early Christian believers. He had inherited and studied the glorious wisdom of his ancestors. He had reveled in the law. His passion for his religious knowledge drove him to kill and imprison Christians. He thought he pleased God by eradicating this dangerous new contagion.

But after he met Jesus and surrendered to him, Paul realized that the best the Jews and the Greeks had to offer was utter nonsense compared to God's revelation in Christ. In one seemingly preposterous act—the death of Christ on the cross—God had obliterated "the wisdom of the world."

The world's scholars and philosophers scoffed at the cross and ridiculed the proposition that God had redeemed humanity by Christ's sacrifice. But while men and woman laughed at the cross, God had the last laugh. Paul saw through the imposing structure of religious philosophy and speculation. He rightly discerned that the best of human wisdom could never accomplish his salvation and eternal life.

When Paul, a dedicated scholar himself, compared what he had learned with what God had given to him in Jesus his lord, he turned the tables upside down. God's so-called foolishness really was wiser than man's wisdom.

Paul saw this truth not as something theoretical to be debated in the halls of academia. He saw it borne out in the streets of Corinth. When he surveyed the Corinthian believers gathered around him, he must have smiled at God's foolishness. What a crew they were! Not a huge bunch of scholars, nobles, captains of industry, and influence and power brokers.

Most of Paul's companions in the faith stood at the bottom rung of the social, political, business and religious ladder. They didn't even exist in the eyes of the high and mighty. But God took them and held them up to the world to expose the world's folly. All of the world's wisdom put together was helpless when it came to changing the lives of these people in the Corinthian church.

To these people, receiving God's wisdom meant putting their faith, trust, and hope in the power of the cross, which the public at large regarded as foolishness. Simply put, Paul preached the cross so that those who believed would be saved, regardless of who they were (both Jews and Gentiles) and regardless of their current lifestyles.

"We preach Christ crucified," Paul boldly declared in the face of both Jewish religion and Greek philosophy. "I resolved to know nothing while I was with you except Jesus Christ and him crucified."

Paul knew God's power in Jesus for himself and for all who believe. The genuinely wise folks are those who are "in Christ Jesus." To see God's wisdom one must see and understand and believe that Jesus is righteousness, holiness, and redemption—in spite of his ignominious death on the cross.

Paul expounded as truth what he had once stumbled over. He catapulted from human wisdom to God's wisdom, from the wise to the foolish, from the strong to the weak. But out of his weakness poured the stunning power of the cross of Jesus.

Human wisdom constantly seeks to dislodge God's wisdom in our hearts, minds, and wills. But once we choose Jesus to be our lord and savior, as Paul did, he calls us to choose him every day in all the decisions that confront us. God's wisdom in Christ crucified is always our best choice.

To make the wisest choices, we have to grasp the logic of Paul's argument in defense of God's wisdom in the cross. Day by day we discover that

The Supremacy of the Cross

the apparent foolishness of the cross empowers us to be faithful to Jesus and to serve the needs of others.

The Power of the Cross

Philippians 3:12–14; Colossians 2:13–15

Stepping it off around the park one afternoon on my usual path, I was nearly flattened by a horde of guys clad in shorts, jerseys, and sneakers. They thundered around the bend like they meant business, so I quickly dodged out of their way. Once the front-runners disappeared, I got back on the track and met the panting stragglers in this high school cross-country race. From across the way arose the cheers of their screaming teammates, urging these desperately dragged out boys not to quit.

In Paul's day Greek athletes fiercely competed for a simple laurel wreath. Foot-races preceded the other four events of the pentathlon. Olympic athletes swore by Zeus to follow ten months of strict training.

Paul pushed himself to the limit to win the prize for which God had called him. He told Timothy that he had fought the good fight, he had finished his race and so he anticipated receiving his crown from Jesus. For Paul, Christ's cross guaranteed victory, not defeat.

There is no athletic metaphor for something like this. Paul returned to the dreadful scene of mighty Roman legions bringing their chain-ganged captives into the city for their victory celebration. Then he looked at the cross of Jesus. Jesus had taken the worst that hell could throw at him. He threw off the powers of darkness like so much dirty laundry. Beyond that, Paul saw Jesus making a public spectacle of these discarded cosmic powers and led them as captives in his triumphal parade.

On his way to Christ's victory celebration Paul engaged the powers of religion, politics, business, academics, and entertainment. These powers think they are invincible, but Paul saw every power and authority subject to Christ and the power of his cross.

Paul realized that enormous risks confronted him if he lost sight of Jesus on his cross. His cross had to be central in everything Paul did and taught. Paul's vision anticipated the words of the familiar hymn that tells us the cross of Jesus towers over the wrecks of time.

The cross compelled Paul to enlist in the Jesus cause in the first place. The cross guaranteed the outcome of his battles. Submitting to the searchlight of the cross kept Paul in his race. As with Paul, so with us. The cross of Jesus will keep us in our races until we receive our crowns from the Lord Jesus.

If we are to imitate Paul successfully, we must first learn the pattern of his life then follow it. Next, we look at the consistency of his life and teaching, how he used scripture, and what his prayers were like.

CHAPTER 29

His Pattern of Life

In God's wisdom it pleased him to probe deeply into Paul's life so that we would have no doubts about how he lived. So when Paul calls us to imitate him, he also gives us a clear picture of himself. We can only model him when we grasp the basic patterns of his life.

Prototype of Future Believers

1 Timothy 1:12–17

Little did anyone realize that Orville and Wilbur Wright's first aircraft, which flew twelve seconds in 1903, would be the prototype of Boeing 747s and F-16 fighters and B-52 bombers. Likewise, when Paul terrorized Jerusalem no one could have predicted that he would become the prototype of future believers.

Writing to Timothy, his young son in the faith and his faithful coworker, Paul prodded him to keep pursuing God's will with total abandonment. Paul said, in effect, "Timothy, look what God has done for me. He will do the same for you."

Here we see Paul the mentor and coach at his very best. Not ashamed of his sordid past, he drew out of his experience the cardinal confession of Christian faith: Christ Jesus came to save sinners. "Mark it down. You can count on it."

If Timothy possibly had any doubts, Paul went further and took him back to his pre-conversion days when he ravaged the church. Interestingly, Paul said that despite all the havoc he had wreaked against believers, Jesus had still considered him fit for his service.

The prototype of future believers was developed in the real life laboratory of the top-ranked sinner. God, the creator and architect of Paul's life, not only saved him but also gifted him for ministry. As a prototype, therefore, we look to Paul as the example of what God can do for anyone who sees himself or herself as a hopeless case. Beyond that, we also see how God can give a person a significant purpose and mission in life.

Naturally, people like Orville and Wilbur Wright, Thomas Edison, Henry Ford, and Bill Gates properly take credit for developing prototypes that changed the world. On the other hand, Paul changed the world more than all of them put together, but he took no credit for himself. Instead, he credited God's mercy for what had happened to him. The King of all worlds deserves all the glory.

How we meet Jesus is not the critical point. The only resemblance a 747 bears to the Wright brothers' plane is that it flies. The big question Paul posed for Timothy essentially was, "Timothy, are you flying by God's saving mercy?" Today, anyone can take off for heaven by receiving the gift of flight—the boarding pass, as it were—from Jesus.

Consistency of Life and Teaching

2 Timothy 3:10–13

For his protégé Timothy, Paul traced the pattern of his life in forty-four words (2 Tim 3:10–11). Paul and Timothy had worked together so closely that Paul did not need to recount every detail of his life. After all, Timothy was so young that Paul considered him his son. As a son follows his daddy around and copies his habits, so Timothy had copied Paul step by step.

Paul exuded confidence about the consistency of his life and his teaching. He reminded Timothy that there was no difference between what he taught and how he lived. Paul wrote, in effect: "Timothy, you have seen how my life squares with my teaching. Therefore, stand by the truths you have learned and use them for discipline in right living."

What else did Timothy know about his mentor? The overwhelming fact that, in spite of unrelenting persecution, Paul had not surrendered his commission. Perhaps more than anything else, Paul used that fact to spur Timothy forward to fulfill his calling. In other words, "No matter what happens, Timothy, do not quit."

Paul had resolved to keep going in the face of horrendous opposition with faith, patience, love, and endurance. These four anchors stabilized the ship of his life in the face of violent storms. Timothy needed such strong security because of the battles that were sure to come his way.

For Paul, faith was not simply intellectual assent to a set of propositions. Rather, it was the driving force of his life. He endured patiently, with love, because his faith in Jesus knew no limits. He knew Jesus as God incarnate, the person who had died for his sins. But he also knew him as the creator and sustainer of the universe. He enjoyed valid reasons for trusting Jesus in the fires of persecution.

Paul's brief sketch of his life instructed and inspired Timothy by encouraging him to trust Jesus for strength, hope, and courage in the days to come. "What God did for me," Paul said, in effect, "he can and will do for you. Act on what you have seen to be true in my life."

Paul gives the same wise counsel to us. Look around and see what God has done for his faithful servants in your lifetime. Learn from them and follow them step by step. In our spiritual pilgrimage following Paul, we need faith, love, and endurance, not just to survive but to win.

HIS USE OF SCRIPTURE

2 Timothy 3:14–17

Did Paul read through his Bible once a year? Did he use a devotional guide for his daily quiet time with God? How did he use his Bible (the Old Testament), which he read in Greek and Hebrew? We can't read our devotional habits into Paul's time, but he did leave us ample evidence of how he used his Bible.

Paul's Bible knowledge began at home, where he grew up as a Pharisee. Then he studied at Gamaliel's school in Jerusalem. Along the way, he acquired an encyclopedic knowledge of the Old Testament. Such wisdom he used skillfully later on in his preaching, teaching, and correspondence. For example, in his letters and sermons he cited Genesis twenty-seven times.

For him, the Old Testament was packed with warnings about how to live (1 Cor 10:11; Rom 15:4). Therefore, his knowledge of Israel's history proved the validity of the moral and ethical applications he made to the church. Beyond that, he interpreted the prophets to point to Jesus. The mysteries hidden from the prophets had been solved by Jesus. Paul excelled in unifying Old and New Testament truth.

The Imitation of Saint Paul

In Paul's classic charge to Timothy he pointed to the holy scriptures as the source of personal salvation and the guide for Christian teaching and living. He attributed the power of his Bible to God's breath, a remarkable insight that gives divine authority to Christian teaching. Paul did not tell Timothy exactly how God breathed into the writers of his Bible. By faith he trusted that what he held in his hands, and that the truth he taught from it originated with God Almighty. Such confidence kept him on course in fulfilling Christ's mission.

Of course Paul turned to Christ when he was an adult, whereas Timothy had been brought up in the Bible. After his conversion Paul searched "all scripture" to find what he needed for himself and for his converts. God's word had rebuked, corrected, and trained him along the way. For this to happen he maintained disciplined study and worship habits.

From both the scope and depth of Paul's Old Testament references, we know he must have been meticulous about keeping up his reading and study. His letters reveal knowledge of much more than Israel's history. For example, his seventy allusions to the Psalms show that he opened himself to God in worship and prayer according to Israel's guide. It's hard to imagine anyone more thoroughly saturated with God's truth than he was.

Therefore, he advised the Ephesian Christians to fight with the Holy Spirit's sword, God's word. Paul used the Bible as part of God's strategic weaponry for spiritual warfare. It was much more than a storehouse of religious knowledge. The Bible gave Paul wisdom, courage, and perseverance. Confident of God's plan, he endured hardships in faith, clinging to the truths of scripture.

Paul best epitomized Jeremiah's testimony that he ate God's word and it was a fire in his bones. That's how I like to picture Paul, a man who consumed God's word and in turn was consumed by it.

Paul left us with a witness that without God's word informing and training us, we are useless ciphers in God's account books. To imitate Paul, we must be filled with the knowledge of scripture so that we can glorify God and enrich the lives of others.

Holy, Righteous, Blameless

1 Thessalonians 2:10

Paul claimed that the Thessalonian believers and God himself could testify to his godly, righteous, irreproachable life. What did that look like for Paul when he visited that city, preaching the gospel, working as a tentmaker, and nurturing new believers? Generally, we surmise that he didn't lose his temper when someone rubbed him the wrong way. Although he mixed with pagans, he did not participate in their debaucheries. He was kind, generous, sympathetic, patient, and longsuffering.

Demonstrating holiness, righteousness, and blamelessness as a tentmaker, Paul did honest, quality work. He did not cheat his customers. He kept his head about him and respected people who came his way. He stayed clear of those who made and sold shoddy goods. He never joined the guild of artisans in their bawdy jokes, parties, and drunkenness.

As a preacher and teacher, he did not exalt himself. He stayed with the simple, clear truths of the gospel. He did not depend on his eloquence or persuasiveness. He did not entice people with false promises.

Paul would be the last person to claim that he had no imperfections. Rather, while he worked at his trade and while he taught the church his chief concern was that nothing in his life and demeanor would bring disgrace to Jesus and the gospel, and that nothing would be an obstacle to anyone hearing and learning the gospel. Paul knew that he had to be a model in word and in conduct, living an exemplary life for the advance of the gospel and the growth in moral and spiritual development among Christians.

As best he knew, his character reflected something of God's holiness and righteousness. Because Jesus lived in him, and he was united with Christ in his death, burial and resurrection, he was freed from sin's power. As far as he could tell, his life style brought no reproach ("blameless") on Jesus and the church.

In his letters Paul did not hide his personal struggles. He fought against sin and resisted the devil. He saw his life as a journey toward Christlikeness and perfection. He set high standards for himself and the church. He knew that the Holy Spirit produced fruit that pleased God. As Christians, we strive as Paul did, to make our conduct match our confession of faith, to make sure our practice is consistent with our position in Christ.

Magnificent in Prayer

Ephesians 1:15–23

Paul's story in Acts does not depict him in personal prayer times. To find out how he prayed, we read his letters. Most of them reveal a person magnificent in prayer. So magnificent, in fact, that our own prayers appear decrepit alongside his.

Paul's prayers grab us in the opening verses of Romans, Ephesians, Philippians, Colossians, 1 and 2 Thessalonians, 2 Timothy, and Philemon. Their passion and scope expose Paul as one who intensely desired God's highest and best for his sisters and brothers in Christ. He appears like a mother pouring out her heart to God Almighty for the sake of her children.

Paul not only instructed us to pray, he also modeled how it's done. "Pray without ceasing" patterned his life. "Pray with thanksgiving" set the tempo of his prayers. He urged "that requests, prayers, intercession and thanksgiving be made for everyone" (1 Tim 2:1). He laid it on men especially "to lift up holy hands in prayer, without anger or disputing" (1 Tim 2:8).

I attached the adjective "magnificent" to Paul's prayers because they transform banal prayers into something dynamically life-changing. They are like the infusion of fresh blood into a surgical patient.

For the development of our prayer concerns, we can compare them with some of Paul's. For example, he prayed for the Ephesians to know God better. He prayed that they would experience God's gift of hope and the wealth of their inheritance in Christ. He wanted them to live with the same power that raised Christ from the dead. In our prayers we can be transported from our daily routines and the multitude of our problems to grasp the awesome power of Jesus who reigns supreme over all authorities everywhere.

Something similar marked his prayer for the Colossians (1:9–14). He prayed for their spiritual wisdom and understanding. He asked God to give them lives completely pleasing to him, full of fruit, good works, and thankfulness. He prayed for an abundance of patience and endurance.

Sometimes, as with the Romans, he simply reminded them of how constantly he prayed for them. Or, he dropped in a gracious word of thankfulness for his partnership with the Philippians. He brought before the Lord the work, faith, endurance, and love of the Thessalonians. He wanted them to find fulfillment in God's purpose, that Jesus would be glorified in them. He assured Timothy that he prayed for him night and day. He thanked God for Philemon's love and faith and asked that he might actively share his faith.

Such prayers transcended pious platitudes. Paul brought to God both personal and corporate needs. The body of Christ as a whole needs Paul's kind of prayers, as much as individuals do. Our prayer concerns rightly begin at home, with our own needs and those of our families and friends. But, as with Paul, we must grasp the larger picture of prayer as part of God's plan for the church and the world. We join hands and hearts with our sisters and brothers to make sure our mutual spiritual needs stand foremost in our prayers.

Our next chapter touches the raw nerves of sorrow and anxiety that Paul endured. How he faced them establishes the way we can follow him and find contentment as he did.

CHAPTER 30

Sorrow, Anxiety, and Contentment

How thankful we are that Paul bared his heart and soul in matters that touch us so intimately. He did not teach and write as someone tightly wrapped in insulation like a power cord. Even in grief and anxiety, however, he clasped the hands of Jesus and found comfort and contentment.

Grief over a Brother

Philippians 2:19–30

Sorrow and anxiety constitute the fabric of our lives. No one escapes. Likewise, Paul was not immune to them either. As with us, his sorrow grew out of a great friend's illness to the point of death. When God in his mercy healed and spared Epaphroditus, he also saved Paul from "sorrow upon sorrow."

Had Epaphroditus died, Paul would have grieved because of his loss. This man, of whom we know little, had so endeared himself to Paul that he would have mourned deeply. Somehow, we do not think of Paul as a "man of sorrows, and acquainted with grief," as Jesus was (Isa 53:3, KJV). Probably, this is because Paul spoke so eloquently and triumphantly about his Christian hope. He often expressed his desire to die and be with Jesus. He admonished Christians not to grieve as the pagans do, who have no hope. Resurrection and eternal life firmly anchored him.

But here Paul looked at the potential loss of his "brother, fellow worker and fellow soldier," and it hurt. Neither he nor Epaphroditus feared death.

They anticipated seeing Jesus, and yet Paul would weep because he loved this man so much. Epaphroditus linked Paul with his church in Philippi. He had come from these believers to join and serve Paul in his Roman prison, bringing personal goods that sustained him.

Therefore, Epaphroditus was family and the thought of losing him drove Paul to prayer and grief. Death would terminate Paul's prison companionship. It would mean hardship as well as sorrow. Death would sever the apostle's lifeline with Philippi.

But what about Paul's anxiety? Why was he anxious in this affair? This is the man who told us not to be anxious about anything (Phil 4:6). However, like us, he suffered anxiety because a loved one was critically ill. We pray loved ones will pull through and are relieved when they do. Paul felt the same way, but he also experienced godly anxiety over the restoration of the link between Rome and Philippi in the person of Epaphroditus.

The Christians would be greatly relieved to learn that their messenger had survived. Epaphroditus was upset because Philippi had heard he was ill. Paul was anxious to send him back so that their concerns might be relieved. His safe arrival would also comfort Paul, even though it cost him his companion. Simply put, Paul's anxiety grew out of his great heart for the church. It was right to be concerned about their welfare. Doubtless, prayer mitigated the intensity of his anxiety, as it does for us.

Psalm 103:14 cemented itself in Paul's psyche: "He remembers that we are dust." He was not impervious to sorrow and anxiety, but neither did these common frailties debilitate him. He did not wallow in grief over what looked like the end for Epaphroditus. Therein lies the difference for him and for all Christians.

Somehow, in the chill of looming loss, Paul discovered the warmth of God's mercy. We cannot dodge the bullets of illness and death, but when sorrow and anxiety engulf us we can find peace, joy, and security from the Lord. Sometimes our companions are spared, as Epaphroditus was in this case, and in that we find incomparable relief.

Paul knew, as we do, that in the valley of the shadow of death, our good shepherd Jesus takes our hands and safely guides us through. As he did for Paul, God gives us hope and security in our emergencies. God is our refuge and strength, our rock and fortress. To imitate Paul, we put our trust and hope in our Savior's love and care.

The Imitation of Saint Paul

Cure for Anxiety

Philippians 4:6–10

Antidepressant use in the US doubled in the decade between 1996 and 2005, researchers reported. Apparently Americans have resorted to pills in huge quantities in their efforts to assuage depression. Although anxiety does not necessarily lead to depression, it certainly can contribute to it.

On the other hand, Christians have long maintained that Jesus is largely ignored in peoples' efforts to curb anxiety and depression. This despite the fact that he told us to control worry because it doesn't add to either the quality or quantity of life. He promised peace to his followers as well as tribulation. Those in his time who knew their Bibles relied on prophets' promises like Isaiah 26:3: "Thou wilt keep him in perfect peace, whose mind is stayed on thee, because he trusteth in thee" (KJV).

In many circumstances anxiety clung to Paul like flypaper. However, his letters do not reveal him to be a chronic worrier. Anxious? Yes. Worried? No. He was anxious about the health of his churches, the stubborn refusal of his countrymen the Jews to repent and believe the gospel, the welfare of his coworkers. He did not travel from city to city in something like a spiritual Popemobile, shielded from the ordinary cares of spiritual and physical life. The apostle Paul was not one to overlook the God component when it came to dealing with anxiety. He knew and used both the prophetic and the Jesus way.

In his closing thoughts to the Philippians he sounded something like the commanding general of an army, firing orders right and left. All soldiers awaiting the order to charge into battle face nervous anxiety. No officer in his right mind tells them not to be scared and anxious. But that's exactly what Paul did.

Or did he? When he told them not to be anxious he gave them a pointed reminder that it was possible for Christians not to be controlled by worry and anxiety. This was not theory with Paul. That was how he lived.

Of course, our big question for Paul is, How did you do it? How did you live with anxiety but not fall captive to it? His answer is both simple and practical. Pray and let God's peace guard your heart and your mind.

Praying with thanksgiving is one of Paul's toughest assignments. Can I really say Thank You to God when the world's cares and troubles seem to have swallowed me? The waves of cares are simply too powerful and I'm plunged into despair. Drowning in worry and anxiety seems to be my fate.

Paul counsels us to keep on praying and praising God, even when our emotions are not in it. "I don't feel like it" is our greatest hindrance to thankfulness and petition. Or, as Jesus might say, "Keep on drinking of the water of life I offer you."

Reflecting on Paul's life, we are struck by how often he refreshed and restored his soul in prayer and thanksgiving. He did not paper over his worries, but gave them to God. Paradoxically, he knew God's peace which he could not understand. That is the Christian answer to the dilemma of anxiety: God is true, God is real, God in Christ sets a guard over our hearts and minds.

Paul would say, "Don't ask me how it works. It works because of who God is and what he is like. Trust him to protect and shield you from the devastating inroads of anxiety. Instead of chewing your cud of worry, digest the excellent food of truth, purity, love, and grace."

To follow Paul, we must increase our intake of God's peace in Christ. As we confess our bouts of anxiety that threaten to cripple our walk with Jesus, we ask God to help us find in him all we need to overcome our fears and worries.

Inexplicable Contentment

Philippians 4:10–20

Life's journey takes us through peaks and valleys, gains and losses, joys and sorrows. As Christians, our faith teaches us that God's wise and loving providence nurtures us in life's rough patches. Yet sometimes contentment slips through our fingers like a wiggly fish. We find it hard to say amen to Paul's bold avowal that he found contentment in life's highs and lows. Imitate Paul "whatever the circumstances"? Very difficult indeed.

Paul wrote to the Philippians to tell them that he was all right, even though he sat in a Roman prison. Somehow, their gift had gotten through to him after what had seemed like a long delay. Paul seized the opportunity, not just to say thank you, but also to teach a profound spiritual reality.

Imagine sitting in Starbucks in Philippi with your friends and reading his letter together. Questions pop up from all quarters: "Is Paul, okay? How's he getting along? Did he get our gift? What about his trial?" Dare we ask if any of them inquired about Paul's spiritual strength? Did anyone ask if his faith had buckled under pressure?

Earlier in his letter, Paul had assured them that the gospel was advancing in Rome in spite of adverse circumstances (Phil 1:12). Before signing off he addressed their fears for his overall personal welfare. The Philippians probably choked when they read his closing words. Tears welled up in their eyes when he said he was more than all right, he was actually contented.

Had I been there, I would have felt a knife plunging into my heart. Paul contented? How can that possibly be true? If he is contented in prison, why am I griping and complaining about my aches and pains, my children, my boss, some of my fellow believers? I would have swallowed hard under the Holy Spirit's conviction.

Twice Paul explained that he had had to learn contentment. His schooling in contentment had taken him through all circumstances. Instruction covered living in both need and abundance, in hunger and with good meals. He wrote, "I have been very thoroughly initiated into the human lot with all its ups and downs" (vs. 12, NEB).

We say, "Yes, Paul, I can be contented when my belly is full, but I'm not so sure about when I'm starving." Our problem is that too often we identify contentment, or happiness, in terms of our physical well-being. Paul said, in effect, you have to learn happiness "in any and every situation."

As quickly as Paul's readers scratched their heads and asked, "How can this be true"? Paul revealed his secret in two stages: First, there was the power of the risen Christ living in him. "I have strength for anything," he said, "through him who gives me power" (Phil 4:13, NEB). Second, there was the kind practical assistance sent to him by his sisters and brothers at Philippi.

When hardships assail us and we start to feel sorry for ourselves, it's time to draw on our resources in Christ and to accept offers from friends who desire to help us. We conquer both peaks and valleys with Jesus right beside us and with unbreakable bonds of fellowship and support from fellow believers.

With Jesus and our friends, we too can find contentment in good days and bad. Jesus is more than sufficient for anything life throws at us. As he did for Paul, so Jesus will also fill us with his grace and peace when we feel overwhelmed.

Paul's lifetime ministry lasted about fifteen years and a good chunk of that time he spent in prison. His letters show us the way to real freedom in Christ, even though we may never suffer imprisonment. How he handled life as a prisoner is coming up in our next chapter.

CHAPTER 31

Imprisoned for the Gospel

I've never been in prison. The only "confinement" I have faced came while I served in the US Army. People there told you want to do and when, and you had no freedom to disobey. Sometimes in those circumstances I felt like I was in jail. However, compared to Paul's life, my experience was like a minor headache. How refreshingly honest Paul was when he wrote what it meant to be Christ's prisoner.

Ambassador in Chains

Philippians 1:12–18

Paul first tasted chains in Philippi (Acts 16:19–34). Years later, imprisoned in Rome, he assured the Philippians that his chains had not hindered the gospel but had helped it to advance. They doubtless recalled how his imprisonment in their city had also furthered the gospel and led to the establishment of their church.

Chains provide a macabre motif to Paul's life and letters. So much so that he called himself an ambassador in chains (Eph 6:20). Paul first appears in the story of the church as the terror of Christians who threw them into prison. But having helped to turn the Roman world upside down, this bold and courageous preacher and teacher later languished in prison himself.

Paul willingly carried the stigma of chains, knowing they were an embarrassment to some but not to Onesiphorus (2 Tim 1:16). While a prisoner in Caesarea, he dramatically appealed to King Agrippa: "I pray God that not only you but all who are listening to me today may become what I am, except for these chains" (Acts 26:29).

He did not brag about his chains; neither did he hide them when it was necessary to cite what he had suffered for the cause of Christ and the work of evangelism. He did not elaborate to the Ephesians what it meant to be an ambassador in chains, but gave a full explanation to the Philippians.

Rather than restrain Paul, his chains served to spread the story of Jesus throughout the Roman headquarters and the public at large. His chains also inspired other believers to summon courage to speak fearlessly for Christ. Reflecting on the entire experience in a Roman prison, Paul concluded that his chains were worth it because Christ was set forth.

Such also was Paul's experience early on when he was arrested in Jerusalem and then packed off to Caesarea. Because of his chains, he testified to the crowds and religious authorities, then to the Roman governor Felix and the puppet King Agrippa. Finally, under house arrest for two years in Rome, he taught about Jesus openly and without hindrance (Acts 28:30–31). He authenticated his ambassadorship.

Considering imprisonment a privileged position radically changed Paul's outlook. "Ambassador in chains" is an oxymoron, unless we see the positive spin Paul put on it. While his chains restrained him physically, they energized him spiritually because he fiercely executed his commission from Jesus. Jesus had told Paul that he would suffer, so suffering went hand in hand with spreading the gospel. Prison itself became a powerful springboard to the liberation of those imprisoned by sin.

Truth in Jesus sets us free; his truth is not bound by chains. Since Paul's time, prisons have been choked with Christian prisoners who have testified to their faith and led fellow prisoners and guards to Christ.

A huge portion of God's truth belongs to us because Paul wrote letters from prison. Paul turned prison into a holy sanctuary, singing, praying, and talking incessantly about Jesus. Whatever confinement may mean to us, we can choose self-pity, complaint, and despair, or we can rejoice and let our lights shine for Jesus the way Paul did.

Paul's example instructs us both to keep our faith and to tell it to others, even under adverse circumstances. Because we are more likely to complain when our freedoms are curtailed in some way, we need to review Paul's model again and again. Jesus commanded his followers to look after those in prison. Our freedom in Christ compels us to pray for the thousands of imprisoned Christians around the world.

Fearful and Fearless

Ephesians 6:19–20

Paul's astonishingly graphic picture of the fully-armed Christian warrior (Eph 6:10–18) suddenly dissolves into a prayer for fearlessness, boldness, and courage in revealing the gospel. If there ever was a mismatch, this is it. How could the warrior apostle confess his fear and lack of courage and boldness, especially since he had spoken boldly for two years at Ephesus (Acts 19:8–10)?

Because he knew intimately his enemy's prevailing power. Paul was no stranger to the worst kind of wickedness and terror. Political and religious foes brought to bear their might to suppress the man and his message about a new king and emperor, Jesus Christ, who had risen from the dead. Yes, Paul held the rank of ambassador in Christ's diplomatic corps, but he held absolutely no diplomatic immunity. Paradoxically, he was an ambassador in chains.

Paul also knew himself. He possessed no innate powers of persuasion. He could claim no friendly contacts in high places. He totally lacked any influence where it counted in the world's power structure. He had thrown away all his claims to recognition for the sake of knowing Jesus. Inside, he feared he might fail Jesus. He readily admitted his weaknesses, claiming only Christ's power.

He was so unsure of himself that he asked God to give him the right words to say. He claimed no rhetorical skills, no clever arguments. In fact, he knew what he said about Jesus was regarded as stupid and foolish. No one with half a brain would believe his words.

Paul's twice repeated request for fearless, bold words shows that when the test came to declare Jesus there was always the terrible possibility that he might flinch from the whole gospel and cut some corners to make his message more palatable. Nothing has changed in that regard. Every Christian faces that test.

Paul asked for prayer because he was vulnerable and was not ashamed to admit to his Ephesian readers (and us) that he, too, could be chicken when in a tight spot. How much better to admit that the popular teacher and evangelist in Ephesus also needed courage and wisdom to speak up for Jesus at the right time.

There was no good or safe time to tell the Jesus story. Paul knew that at any moment he might be called upon to declare his faith, certainly at the risk of his life. We will fail if we wait for that more convenient, safer time to utter a peep for Jesus. God springs opportunities for us to say something when we least expect it. Such sudden openings demand courage, boldness, and wisdom—what we really lack, if we're honest. That's why Paul's request for prayer must be ours as well.

Every chance to confess Jesus in a hostile environment strikes fear in our hearts. It was the same for Paul, and he did not ask to be delivered from that kind of normal fear. He wanted to say the right words about Jesus so the good news of the gospel, under the Holy Spirit's ministry, might be made clear to pagan hearts and minds.

Paul's example shows us how to win the battle over fear when confronted by an open door for telling someone about Jesus. God knows how hard it is to stand for Christ in the face of possible hostility and ridicule. We pray, as Paul did, for courage, love, and wisdom, and the ability to trust God to bring us safely through such encounters.

LESSONS FROM PRISON

2 Timothy 4:9–18

Two powerfully effective Christian writers of the twentieth century spoke to us from their prison experiences. Dietrich Bonhoeffer, a German Lutheran pastor, was imprisoned by the Nazis and ultimately executed. But before he died he wrote *Letters and Papers from Prison*, which continues to influence Christians today. Likewise, Alexander Solzhenitsyn, a Russian Orthodox believer, during his time in a Siberian labor camp, challenged the communist regime and inspired millions around the world by writing *The Gulag Archipelago*.

Luke the historian in Acts recounted Paul's prison experiences at Philippi, Caesarea, and Rome. Paul learned and taught many lessons from his prison time, which he included in his Prison Epistles: Ephesians, Colossians, Philippians, and Philemon. He wrote 2 Timothy while in prison awaiting his execution.

During his brief incarceration at Philippi, Paul's faith, hope, courage and confidence shone as brightly as a coal miner's lamp 300 feet below the surface. Despite having been flogged and being fastened to stocks in the

Imprisoned for the Gospel

inner prison, he and Silas, his cellmate, sang their praises to God. Later in Rome, because his unquenchable optimism prevailed, he preached Christ to his guards. He was not just another prisoner, but an ambassador of Christ.

During his Roman imprisonment, he described to the Philippians his supreme joy despite his adverse circumstances. Whatever his physical condition and limitations, Paul's sense of joy filled the pages of his letter to them. He accepted suffering as part and parcel of his commitment to Christ. Graphically, he pictured himself as being poured out as a sacrificial offering, yet he urged his readers to "be glad and rejoice with me" (Phil 2:18).

Prison taught Paul "to be content whatever the circumstances" (Phil 4:11). He learned he could "do everything" through Jesus who strengthened him (Phil 4:13). With Jesus with him in prison, Paul found endurance and patience as well as irrepressible joy and contentment.

From prison Paul carried on his teaching via his letters. He reminded the Colossians, "For though I am absent from you in body, I am with you in spirit and delight to see how orderly you are and how firm your faith in Christ is" (Col 2:5). In prison, Paul set his mind on things above, not on earthly things, confident that his life in Christ was safe with God. Christ's words profoundly enriched him.

Supremely, Paul was at peace in prison. Although he hoped and prayed for his release, he did not chafe to be free, nor resent his time there as wasted. He did not complain to God or to his fellow Christians about his miserable fate. Rather, he reminded Philemon that he was not a prisoner of Rome, but of Jesus Christ, and he was in chains for the gospel (Phlm 1, 9, 13). God blessed him with the fellowship of other Christian prisoners and with the assistance of Luke, Onesimus, the runaway slave, and Onesiphorus. But he was stung when no one showed up in court to defend him.

He urged Timothy not to be ashamed of him in prison, but to join him in suffering for the gospel. Persecution will come to all who live godly lives. While he calmly awaited his death, he urged Timothy to visit him quickly before winter, and to bring with him Paul's books and notebooks, a heavy coat, and one-time deserter Mark. Out of his prison cell, he shouted, "Glory to God for ever and ever!"

Although prison may not befall everyone, Paul's Everest-like examples guide us through our confining experiences, so that we too might rejoice in them with patience, courage and hope, and thus be ambassadors for Jesus to a watching world. In a true heart sense, Paul was delivered while chained. He kept on believing in God's goodness, love, and wisdom. His path can be ours as well.

Paul's letters were one of the rich outcomes of his imprisonment. In the next chapter we develop what he had to say from prison about the security of his deposit of faith, his heavenly prize, and the work of God's grace in his life.

CHAPTER 32

Deposit of Faith

Paul's deposit of faith included many assets, of which we can touch on only a few. His security in Christ was a major asset, as was his commitment to "win the prize for which God has called us heavenward." As he reflected on his guaranteed "seat" in heaven, Paul rehearsed how he had received the gift and what was consequently expected of him.

Kept Safe by Jesus

2 Timothy 1:1–12

Paul knew what it was to fear the specter of judgment. He had worked feverishly to secure God's eternal pleasure, carefully fulfilling the law's righteous demands. But then he realized that no matter how much religious and moral wealth he accumulated, none of it would satisfy God.

Taking the patriarch Abraham as his model, Paul underwent a radical reorientation of this thinking. God had declared Abraham righteous by virtue of his faith, not because of his attempts to placate God and earn salvation. Paul discovered what theologians call "imputed" righteousness, that is, God's gift of righteousness to all who trust in his Son, the Lord Jesus Christ.

When Paul discarded his past efforts to please God as so much garbage, he chose faith in Christ instead. Jesus came to live in him and to rule his life. In return, Paul entrusted his life to Jesus as an eternal deposit in the bank of heaven.

Jesus had taught that nothing can touch our faith deposits in heaven. He talked about the threats of moths, rust, and thieves. To that we can add all the ups and downs on the stock market and the values of our homes.

Paul found his eternal security in heaven. He wrote to Timothy out of the suffering of his imprisonment. Under those devastating circumstances, darkness and doubt threatened to overwhelm his soul.

Was Timothy worried about Paul's endurance of physical suffering? Did he wonder about the endurance of his faith? Perhaps so. Paul went to great lengths to assure him that he was all right on both counts.

Nothing could be stronger than Paul's affirmation. From his dark cell these words shined like a mighty lighthouse beacon over troubled waters. Whatever doubt and despair he may have felt, they dissolved under the penetrating brilliance and assurance he found in the Lord Jesus. He was absolutely sure that his faith in Jesus had not been displaced, and that Jesus would never let him down. His deposit of faith with Jesus would never decline in value. He feared no loss of everything he had entrusted to Jesus.

Jesus had died and gone to heaven. Paul saw him as his daily protector and provider. Because he knew Jesus so intimately, Paul spent his last years secure in the knowledge that the day of judgment would pass in his favor. "That day" held no terror for Paul, because his deposit with Jesus guaranteed his acceptance by God.

Paul's faith transaction with Jesus stood solid, no matter what happened to him. Since his soul was secure for eternity, why worry about prison and what the Romans might do to him?

Daniel Whittle in 1883 turned Paul's striking confession into a favorite hymn, called "I Know Whom I Have Believed." When our security begins to slip, we can sing the chorus to powerfully remind us of Jesus who guards our faith deposit in him. Like Paul, we need not be overcome by fear and worry about the future. When Jesus is strong in our lives, our faith will stand like the rock of Gibraltar.

Heavenly Prize

Philippians 3:12–14

The prospect of winning a prize never seriously motivated me. In whatever task I was given, I simply tried to do my best. Whenever I received a prize, therefore, it was unexpected but appreciated. One that shows up

Deposit of Faith

occasionally when we are looking for something else is a small silver tray, the prize I received for writing the best newspaper stories about the sport of skeet shooting.

Likewise, Paul did not preach and teach to win prizes for his oratorical skills, or for making the most converts, or for building the biggest churches. Apparently awards for service never entered his mind as a reason for doing what he did.

Paul enlisted in the Jesus band as a servant, a bond slave of the Lord Jesus Christ. When he signed on, he did so without any promises of prizes or rewards. He followed Jesus because Jesus had changed him from being a self-centered, self-righteous religious bigot to being a humble, Christ centered evangelist.

Paul dropped his old pattern of trying to please God and win rewards with his works of religious zeal. His radical encounter with Jesus provided a revolutionary perspective on rewards, prizes, and goals. Suddenly, Paul changed his focus from earth to heaven. Nothing he might accumulate on earth, be it money or self-righteous zeal, could even match the rewards he had found in Jesus Christ. His accomplishments according to his old religion counted for absolutely nothing compared to his possession of eternal life in Christ.

Paul's old religion guaranteed him nothing in heaven. Jesus changed all that for him. Jesus, king of kings and Lord of lords, sat enthroned with God the Father in heaven. After all, Jesus had promised his disciples future rooms in his heavenly mansion. What a shattering, liberating concept that was for people of the old ways and traditions.

Jesus was personal, not abstract. He lived in Paul. He became the center of Paul's life and the focus of his ministry. The only thing that counted was to please Christ and to receive his prize. Jesus had given Paul a heavenly calling. His calling not only motivated Paul, it also sustained him through beatings, hardships, rejections, and disappointments. When things really got grim, Paul found new inspiration in the prize that awaited him.

Certainly Paul had a lot in his past that he wanted to forget. We can only imagine how difficult that was for him. But somehow he put it all behind him while he pursued the fulfillment of what Jesus had called him to do. Keeping his eyes fixed on Jesus saved Paul from wallowing in his past. His call from heaven kept him firmly on the course that God had plotted for him.

Essentially, Paul committed himself to a heavenly perspective on everything. He rejected earth-bound thinking. Earth-bound thinking leads to competition for prizes that do not last. My little silver tray brings back fond memories, but I do not treasure it and certainly I did not find meaning in life by writing sports stories, enjoyable as that was.

Paul points to the supreme satisfaction of making life a journey toward a heavenly goal. Even with all his achievements, he pictured himself as a pilgrim pursuing a cherished goal. Above everything else, he wanted to please Jesus and to receive his prize. Such a single-minded purpose infuses our lives with meaning and drives us on to be faithful followers of Christ our lord.

We thank God for Paul's motivation for serving Jesus, As we imitate Paul, we can prevent earth-bound thinking from clouding our goal of Christ's prize. It's so easy to slip into pursuing earthly goals that we need Paul's reminder to desire the prize of God's calling in Jesus more than anything else.

Seated in Heaven

Ephesians 2:1–10

Paradoxically, Christians live in heaven now but not yet. Paul saw himself seated with Christ in heaven now, but at the same time he longed to throw off his earthly dwelling and be clothed with his heavenly dwelling. What is mortal must be swallowed up by life.

Paul knew that Jesus Christ had described eternal life as beginning the moment one believes in him, not when we get to heaven. But Jesus also explained that he had prepared dwelling places in heaven for his own. So Paul taught that heaven begins now in the sense of our being united with Christ who lives there at the Father's right hand.

Best of all, Paul's seat in heaven had been allotted to him not because he was worthy of the honor, but because God had given it to him out of pure grace. In fact, Paul was totally undeserving because of the dreadful outworking of his sinful nature. He was spiritually dead, living under God's wrath.

God's great love and rich mercy made Paul alive even when he was dead. With this dramatic transformation came his spiritual resurrection and his exalted position with Christ. At the same time—and here's another paradox with Paul—his supreme desire was to know Christ, share his sufferings, and experience his resurrection power (Phil 3:10).

The crucial question for Paul to answer was how God's love and mercy had become effective in his life, considering the despicable things he had done to God's people. In fact, Jesus told him he was persecuting him.

He had been saved by grace, through faith, which in itself was God's gift. Paul could not possibly have ever accumulated enough good deeds to satisfy God's righteous demands and atone for his sins. Zealous Pharisee that he was, all his religious accomplishments could never gain him his seat in heaven.

My wife and I enjoy summer concerts at Ravinia Park in suburban Chicago. Our resources gain us entrance only to the lawn, so we carry our own lawn chairs. One night, however, a woman appeared out of nowhere and offered us her two seats in the center front section of the orchestra pavilion. For some reason she had to leave the venue and the seats were ours. "Thank you very much," we said and off we went to our prime seats. Nothing we had done earned us those seats. All we had to do was accept the grace offered.

That's how Paul gained his seat with Christ in heaven. By faith he believed what Jesus told him to do and in God's grand, inexplicable plan even his faith was a gift. Paul's life radically changed at that moment. With his seat guaranteed, he received his marching orders and went on to discover the good works God had arranged for him to do. His old zeal returned, but with a new motivation and a new cause.

Paul disproved the old criticism that Christians are so heavenly minded that they are no earthly good. Paul thanked God for the certain hope of heaven to come. In the meantime, he displayed what it means to bring transforming life to people who are dead in their sins. That is the supreme good in anyone's life.

Paul's seat in heaven guaranteed his future and anchored his life in the present. Shock waves of many kinds hit him time and again, but he doggedly persisted in his calling. Because he was sure of heaven, he never backed off from tough assignments.

Paul's seat in heaven changed everything and therefore he eagerly sought God's handiwork in his life. To model Paul, we receive God's grace in Christ by faith and then give ourselves fully to his purposes.

Paul's deposit of faith brought him what the hymn writer called "blessed assurance." Paul was sure of heaven because he had accepted God's grace in Christ. He was determined to serve Jesus faithfully until he received his reward.

One of Paul's major motivating themes was God's glory. We go next to this universal perspective that pervaded his life and ministry.

CHAPTER 33

God's Glory
Paul's Ultimate Purpose

A television travel program took us to Belgium and the city of Antwerp, site of the world's diamond market. We marveled at the skill of the diamond cutters as they produced brilliant light bursting forth from uncut stones. That's a minimal, earthly reflection of what God's glory meant to Paul. His glory encompassed everything in Paul's life.

To the Praise of God's Glory

Ephesians 1:3–14

God's praise and glory were etched on Paul's mind and heart by the divine engraver. So much so that one can hardly turn a page in his letters without encountering God's glory. More than sixty times, in fact.

God's glory burned in Paul's soul because of his intimate knowledge of the Old Testament and his vision of the risen Christ. The God of the Old Testament demanded to be glorified by his people through their obedience to his laws. The Psalms capture the essence of this relationship with repeated calls to glorify, praise and extol the Lord. Paul certainly knew Psalm 57:5 and 11: "Be exalted, O God, above the heavens; let your glory be over all the earth."

On the Damascus Road Paul fell into line with the earlier apostles who had recognized the glory of God in the person of Jesus of Nazareth. Jesus himself clearly established that his glory had originated with God the Father in heaven. That's why Stephen, as he was about to die, exclaimed that he saw God's glory and Jesus at God's right hand.

Two powerful streams merged to shape Paul's passion for God's glory. As a worshiping Jew, he had experienced what God's glory revealed about himself. But majestic as that understanding was, it was magnified a thousand times at least when Paul met Jesus himself.

Paul based his gospel appeal on our falling short of God's glory, that is, his moral perfection, righteousness, holiness, and truth. Grasping this truth opened the floodgates to Paul of the life-changing implications of God's glory. It demands repentance, faith, obedience, and worship.

God's glory shines most brilliantly in our conversion and commitment, of course, but for Paul it also cast light on his future with Christ. Jesus was Paul's lord of glory here and now and also his hope of glory for eternity. When he turned to Jesus, Paul inherited what he called the riches of his glory. No wonder his benedictions ascribe all glory and praise to God.

Lifting up God's glory enabled Paul not only to praise him now and anticipate his future with hope, it also motivated his life and ministry. Once redeemed by Jesus, he strove to do everything to the glory of God. He lived what Jesus taught about people seeing our deeds and thus being drawn to glorify God.

Paul saw his work as the escalation of the revelation of God's glory. The Israelites could not stand to look at Moses because God's glory shined in his face. That glory soon faded, but Paul said his ministry of the Holy Spirit was "even more glorious" (2 Cor 3:8). He called it "surpassing glory . . . which lasts!" He reflected God's glory as he was being changed into God's likeness "with ever-increasing glory" (2 Cor 3:18).

Given these facts, we understand why Paul extolled the praise of God's glory three times in Ephesians 1. Paul saw God in control and history moving toward fulfillment according to God's wisdom and love in Christ. Paul celebrated his sure hope in Christ and consequently his life as praise to God's glory. The person who has confidence in Christ is supposed to bring praise to his glory.

Supremely, Paul sought to see the manifestations of God's glory in the churches he founded. Therefore, the authors of the Westminster Confession of Faith (London, 1646) had it right when they declared that our chief end is to glorify God.

Jesus came in his glory and sits on the throne of his glory. We may not see Jesus as Paul and the apostles did, but with the eye of faith we can be "transfigured into his likeness, from splendor to splendor; such is the influence of the Lord who is Spirit" (2 Cor 3:18, NEB). Out of such experiences grows our passion for God's glory. Like Paul, this passion will both purify and motivate us as we serve the Lord.

Paul strived to make God's glory real in his life. We imitate him when we give priority to God's glory in our thoughts and actions. We confess that we do not glorify God as we should because we spend too much time on ourselves. As we are changed more and more into Christ's likeness, God's glory is truly exhibited and praised. Paul understood that whatever spiritual wisdom and fruit God gives us is for the glory and praise of God.

His Glorious Future

Colossians 1:27; Philippians 2:10–11

Television news reporters rush to the scene of a fire. A mother has lost her child. "How do you feel?" they ask, or something equally inane. The World Series of baseball is over and the reporter asks a player, "What's it feel like to win the Series?" In both cases, their feelings—whether of sorrow or of triumph—are extremely difficult to put into words.

Something like that challenged Paul when he tried to explain God's glory. He knew well the Old Testament stories about the revelation of God's glory to Moses and the Israelites. He knew the tragedy that befell Israel when God's glory departed. But now there is no physical evidence of God's glory for Paul to see.

The Greeks of Paul's time used "glory" (*doxa* in Greek, from which we get our word *doxology*) to express primary values of vital importance. *Doxa* focused on what others said about your actions and achievements. Your fame exalted you above others. The Greeks loved to be praised and honored by others.

However, Paul's idea changed human praise to praise to God. That's because he knew his Greek Old Testament. The translators of Hebrew to Greek used *doxa* to convey something far more compelling than exalted human opinions—the exaltation of God. Because of how God had revealed himself in the history of the Jews, they pictured God as majestic, high and lifted up, and eminently worthy of our praise.

So, although our attempts to describe God's glory fall inadequately short of the reality, as we follow Paul we can see how the concept formed the foundation of his life. For example, Paul looked beyond his immediate suffering and work to the time when he would share Christ's triumphant glory. Living in Christ, he was assured of a glorious future with him. Paul did not describe what Christ's glory would be like. God gave him a glimpse of it and that was enough.

Paul never asked God, "What's in this for me?" Rather, the Holy Spirit revealed to him the glorious future awaiting God's son, the Lord Jesus Christ. As God in the flesh, Jesus had relinquished his divine prerogatives, became a human being, and suffered grievously. In the end, however, he will be glorified when all tongues confess him as lord and all knees bow before his majesty.

For Paul, God's glory assured his future. He lived to the praise of God's glory. Because Jesus lived in him, one day he would see himself and he would understand what God's glory really was all about. Moses asked God to see his glory and God told him to turn his back as he passed by. In Christ, no longer is that necessary.

Paul understood that when Jesus returns he will be glorified in his people. That's why he called Christ's return his "glorious appearing" (Titus 2:13). Paul had learned that one day "men will see the Son of Man coming in the clouds with great power and glory" (Mark 13:26).

To imitate Paul, we must spend time in worship, asking God to be glorious in us. Meditating on the Psalms is a good place to start, followed by some of the glorious scenes pictured in Christ's revelation to John (Rev 4:1–12; 5:12–13).

God's Glory Rules

1 Thessalonians 2:10–12; 1 Corinthians 10:31–33

Jesus said that if we put his kingdom and righteousness first, all we need will be given to us (Matt 6:33). Paul related to that principle when he explained that how we live should be "worthy of God, who has called you into his kingdom and glory." With such a radical idea, he turned the rules of behavior upside down.

God had called Paul to a specific work. He said over and over again that what he did was in response to Christ's command. But far beyond what Paul did was his motive for doing so; he had been called to God's "kingdom and glory."

Whatever he preached and taught, and whatever it cost him to be faithful to Jesus and the gospel, he persevered because he wanted to please, praise and glorify God. He wanted to receive God's approval for everything he did. In effect, he said, "Whatever you do, be sure it magnifies and glorifies God."

This echoes the Psalmist who said God's people will praise and extol him. "They will tell of the glory of your kingdom . . . so that all men may know of your mighty acts and the glorious splendor of your kingdom" (Ps 145:11–12).

Paul recognized that what Jesus did far surpassed the Psalmist's rationale for glorifying God. God's glorious kingdom has been fully incarnated in Jesus. Therefore, Paul was duty bound to bring praise, honor, and glory to God.

To follow Paul here, we consider that his duty to live for God's glory was not just his personal responsibility. He saw God's glory being manifested in the body of believers, the church. The church in service, worship, and witness collectively is called to glorify God. Paul would have us hoist that test over everything our churches do. "Is this really for God's glory?" we ask when contemplating some activity.

To get our arms around Paul's controlling desire to glorify God, we look at some of his benedictions: "To our God and Father be glory for ever and ever" (Phil 4:20). Rhapsodizing about his own conversion, Paul burst forth with: "Now to the King eternal, immortal, invisible, the only God, be honor and glory for ever and ever" (1 Tim 1:17). After a long discussion of God's plan for Israel (Rom 9–11), Paul concluded: "For from him and through him and to him are all things. To him be the glory forever!" (Rom 11:36).

In our concluding chapter, we consider how Paul faced death, grief, and the end of his fight.

CHAPTER 34

Death and Other Endings

One winter my wife and I took an evening course offered by the University of Chicago. It was entitled, "Death and Other Endings." Our professor assured us there was no place for religion in these classes. She wanted to know why we had come and drew from us stories about our losses and the "endings" we had experienced at various stages of our lives.

Several weeks passed and one night a lawyer pronounced that all religion was a fraud. Suddenly, the professor turned to me and asked me to respond. I simply replied that many people did think religion was a fraud, but there were many like me who believed that God had sent his son Jesus Christ to reveal truth, and he was not a fraud.

By the conclusion of the course we had befriended a hurting woman and were able to direct her to some Christian resources for help. Mostly, however, we realized how deep the pain is for those who have no knowledge of what the apostle Paul talked about regarding death

We close this chapter and this book by looking at how Paul viewed the end of his own faith race.

UNDERSTANDING DEATH

2 Corinthians 5:1–10

Death smashed me in the face a couple of times when my first wife died suddenly in childbirth and my sixteen-year-old son drowned. Paul squarely confronted his mortality by looking beyond it to his heavenly immortality. Such an incredible fact stabilized his faith and mine as well.

Death and Other Endings

A sudden longing for heaven did not grip me, but Paul's take on his inevitable demise pointed the way through my gloom like a coal miner's lamp shining in a dark tunnel. Total darkness did not engulf me. Paul showed me that it is possible to contemplate death in a positive way.

Such paradoxical faith does not spare us pain, grief, loss, sorrow, separation, loneliness, and tears. I call it paradoxical because for many people death means the end of everything. Nothing exists for them beyond the grave. How can one escape this desperately dreary prospect? By following Paul's footsteps, anticipating heavenly clothing.

Realistically, we admit with Paul that we live in an "earthly tent" that one day will be destroyed. However, we spare no effort, no expense putting off that event. In our younger years we anticipate living forever; when we get older we feel the day is approaching too fast, too soon. We are not eager to depart our earthly dwelling.

No matter how difficult it may be to face this truth, our Christian faith strongly assures us that our tents will be replaced by an eternal house in heaven, provided by God himself. Earth and heaven analogies figure prominently in the Bible. God's people stand in the middle, so to speak, "groaning," Paul says, to be clothed with their heavenly dwelling. Abraham, the prototype of all tent-dwellers, longed "for a better country—a heavenly one" (Heb 11:16).

Paul offered a striking picture of the tension we all feel. On the one hand, we do not want to shed our old bodies. On the other, we desire to have the new body put on over it, so to speak, "so that our mortal part may be absorbed into life immortal" (2 Cor 5:4, NEB). Our departed loved ones have reached this goal, freed from their earthly-heavenly tension.

God assured our destiny by giving us the Holy Spirit. This fact inspired supreme confidence in Paul. His wisdom shows the way for us. As long as we live physically we live as exiles from the Lord. Christians do not yet see Jesus. In the meantime, we follow him by faith. Living by faith, not by sight, provides security, confidence, and hope when death strikes. Paul's principle steers us through doubt and despair.

With his heavenly dwelling guaranteed, Paul did not waste time worrying about his future. Death threats and risky circumstances accompanied him throughout his life. Whether he lived or died, being acceptable to his commander-in-chief was his priority. He knew that one day death would bring him face to face with Jesus, who would judge his conduct.

Paul grounded his faith in Jesus, who came to deliver his people from bondage to the fear of dying. When Paul met Jesus, he confessed that his life was not his own. He belonged to Jesus, who died and rose again. Consequently, for him to die was gain (Phil 1:21).

Does this mean he lacked an emotional response to death? Was he like an ice sculpture in the midst of grieving friends? Absolutely not. What he called death's sting hurt him as much as anyone else. But he knew that Jesus had promised a heavenly home to his followers (John 14:1–4). Because Jesus defeated death and ascended into heaven, Paul knew for sure where he was headed. The same Holy Spirit who comforted and instructed Paul lives in every follower of Christ. With Paul, we desire to live acceptably to God, whatever span of strength and time it pleases him to give us.

Turning Grief to Joy

1 Thessalonians 4:13–18

Unlike Jesus, we do not see Paul weeping at the grave of a dear friend. Paul's preponderant references to grief in his letters pertain to his grief over possible broken relationships in his church family. Paul admitted to human grief, but not the same kind of grief exhibited by pagans. To Paul, being a Christian makes a difference in how we grieve.

Peter candidly spoke of "grief in all kinds of trials" (1 Pet 1:6). The closest we come to any kind of emotional outlet in Paul's life is his experience with Epaphroditus. The possibility of this "fellow soldier's" death filled Paul with the prospect of "sorrow upon sorrow" (Phil 2:27).

Paul's outlook toward grief undoubtedly was deeply affected by Jesus's teaching that his disciples' grief will be turned to joy. That in itself is a hard pill to swallow. When my wife died in her early thirties, and later on our son died at sixteen, I knew what Paul meant by "sorrow upon sorrow." In that sense, my feelings did not differ from those who suffer similar losses but who are not Christians. Every day, it seems, our Chicago television news programs feature people sorrowing from family losses: children burned to death in a house fire, or, more often, teenagers gunned down in the streets.

Yet Paul believed my grief should somehow differ from universal grief. What did he think was distinctive about Christian grief? He specified one thing: hope. Our pain may be the same, but hope makes a huge difference.

Death and Other Endings

Paul turned grief into hope by asserting the foundational Christian belief in Christ's resurrection and ours. On that great, triumphant day when Jesus comes back with his own he will usher in a reunion like no other. For Christians, the Lord's return means one thing: rejoining our loved ones with Jesus forever.

Rather than speculate on the when and how of this colossal reunion, Paul felt it was much more important to think about our resurrection with Jesus. Our television news reporters rarely find grieving survivors who talk about being with our loved ones and Jesus forever.

I confess that in my grief I did not talk about meeting my wife and son when Jesus returns. I knew they were with Jesus. I knew Jesus loved me. I knew that somehow he would see me through my terrible ordeal. I wept, but I did not weep hopelessly. Even though I could not articulate Paul's vision, it resided deep in my heart and soul.

Paul's stricture not to grieve like pagans must not be taken in isolation. We sense he was aware of the pain of death and separation, because he told the Thessalonians to encourage one another, that is, with Christian hope based on Christ's resurrection and ours. Too often we get tongue-tied when we try to comfort a grieving friend. Meaningful encouragement does not depend on our facility with nice words. It depends on Christ's reality in our presence.

Whatever forms our encouragement takes, we can help to transform someone's grief to joy. The reality of Jesus in our lives is all it takes. Like Paul, we can rivet our attention on future glory that will far surpass the pain we feel now.

Although specific grief counseling seems absent on Paul's agenda, we draw on the plethora of his teachings about Jesus and our hope to sustain us in our sorrows. Because Jesus knew sorrow personally, we face it with him on our side. Paul knew the God of all comfort and through Jesus so do we.

Exalting Jesus in Life and Death

Philippians 1:19–26

Confronting death, Paul talked about Jesus. The man who had hated Jesus and his followers now saw no meaning to life or death apart from him. Such a concern for Jesus gave Paul a dominating single focus and purpose to his life. At the same time, it liberated him from fear of dying.

They say that the gallows focuses your life. Was this how it happened with Paul? Did his imprisonment and impending execution suddenly flood everything else out of his life except Jesus? Perhaps not, because Paul had walked with Jesus. He taught Jesus and suffered for Jesus. He did not make his acquaintance in jail.

As death loomed, Paul drew on his deep knowledge of Jesus. Embedded in Paul's soul, Jesus motivated, inspired, instructed, and encouraged Paul. Like an arctic icebreaker determined to reach open water, Paul drove ahead in his quest to know Jesus and the power of his resurrection and the fellowship of his suffering.

Now he longed to depart this life so he could be with Christ. If he had a choice in the matter, he would choose death and Jesus. Jesus was far better than staying alive. Nevertheless, he sensed that his life could still serve some useful purpose. In Paul, Jesus would sparkle like the stars in the heavens, whether Paul lived or died.

Simultaneously, Paul looked for heaven and for doing good on earth. Not one to resign himself to despair, his focus on Jesus drove him to encourage others. Because the supremacy of Jesus smashed everything else, Paul's prison glowed with the power of the gospel. Paul had lived his life to the full, he was prepared to depart, but in the meantime the incomparable greatness of Christ remained his passion.

The End of the Fight

2 Timothy 4:6–8

Perhaps no lessons in life are as valuable as those we glean at the feet of battle-scarred warriors for Jesus. Incalculable wealth is stored up in their hearts and minds. That's a major reason why God places such a steep price tag on the value of wisdom handed down from generation to generation.

We stand with Paul as the curtain rings down on the drama of his life. He takes center stage for one last time, as it were, and the audience—first Timothy and then the church—leans forward to leach the last drop of power and instruction from the imprisoned apostle.

Paul faced certain execution. Imaginatively, and with Old Testament warrant, he saw himself ready to be offered to God. This man told us that because of God's mercies we're supposed to live like human sacrifices (Rom 12:1–2). Now for him the figure has become reality. He had poured out his life for Jesus and now it was departure time. The departure lounge had closed, the jetway had disengaged, and his plane to heaven was ready for flight.

But there was time for a few final words. What does his wisdom tell us? Life is a fight, a race. It's a battle for faith. Is that what we thought we were getting into when we decided to follow Jesus? Hard to say conclusively, but I suspect that was not what we bargained for at our entry point. When the fight and the race get too hot for us, we too easily retreat to a more comfortable environment.

Struggle for faith? What could that mean, Paul? For him it meant fighting off unrelenting enemies of false religion and exponents of appetizing fleshly desires. Faith is a gift we must protect at all costs. Jesus is worth fighting for with all the strength and resources we can muster.

Reflecting on Paul's battles, we grasp something of his indomitable spirit, inspired wisdom, and heart-stopping courage. Through it all, he sensed that his warfare was not primarily physical but spiritual. Endurance and hope marked his career. He endured opposition, criticism, misunderstanding, and illness. Christ's power within him inspired hope in the eternal. Without his eternal perspective, Paul would have failed.

He fought his battles with profound theological wisdom and insight. He won in the end because he never gave up his convictions about God, the supremacy of the Christ, and the Holy Spirit's abiding presence. At the same time, Paul never hid his emotions. Feelings did not rule his mind, but he loved people. The church was not an abstraction, but a fellowship of living, breathing, hurting, loving people.

We cannot wrap up Paul in a neat package. He lived with conviction of the mind, confidence of the heart, and conduct befitting his calling and God's holiness. He did not back off fights for truth and holiness. If we can put Paul in the arena fighting for one thing it would be the truth of the gospel of God's grace, the truth of salvation by faith alone.

If we had the chance, perhaps we would ask Paul, "What else do you have to tell us, old man?" He would answer: "Just this. I'm going to be crowned by Jesus himself. My battle has been tough and painful, filled with incredible suffering, but his crown will make me forget all that. And if you love him, he will give you a crown, too."

Listening to and imitating Paul causes us to thank God for his triumph. It also causes us to cry out to God that we might finish our lives with a testimony similar to Paul's. May God be pleased and glorified to do that for us.

www.ingramcontent.com/pod-product-compliance
Lightning Source LLC
Chambersburg PA
CBHW020850160426
43192CB00007B/864